Connect with English

Grammar Guide 3

Kathleen F. Flynn • Marilyn Rosenthal • Irwin Feigenbaum • Linda Butler

with contributions by
Michael Berman • John Chapman • Robin Longshaw • Cheryl Pavlik • Jane Sturtevant

McGraw Hill

Boston, Massachusetts   Burr Ridge, Illinois   Dubuque, Iowa   Madison, Wisconsin
New York, New York   San Francisco, California   St. Louis, Missouri
Bangkok   Bogotá   Caracas   Lisbon   London   Madrid   Mexico City·
Milan   New Delhi   Seoul   Singapore   Sydney   Taipei   Toronto

McGraw-Hill

A Division of The McGraw·Hill Companies

CONNECT WITH ENGLISH: GRAMMAR GUIDE BOOK 3

This book is printed on acid-free paper.

7 8 9 BKM BKM 0 9 8 7 6

ISBN-13: 978-0-07-292770-2

ISBN-10: 0-07-292770-4

Editorial director: Thalia Dorwick
Publisher: Tim Stookesberry
Development editor: Pam Tiberia
Marketing manager: Tracy Landrum
Production supervisor: Richard DeVitto
Print materials consultant: Marilyn Rosenthal
Project manager: Shannon McIntyre, Function Thru Form, Inc.
Design and Electronic Production: Function Thru Form, Inc.
Typeface: Frutiger

Grateful acknowledgment is made for use of the following:
Still photography: Jeffrey Dunn, Ron Gordon, Judy Mason, Margaret Storm

Library of Congress Catalog Card No.: 97-75579

TABLE OF CONTENTS

TO THE TEACHER

The primary goal of each *Grammar Guide* is to help students develop mastery of the grammatical structures found throughout the **Connect with English** video episodes. This introduction and the following visual tour provide important information on how each *Grammar Guide* and the corresponding video episodes can be successfully combined to teach English as a second or foreign language.

PROFICIENCY LEVEL:

Designed for beginning through high-intermediate students, *Grammar Guides 1-4* provide a systematic presentation of the basic structures and grammatical features of American English. Examples from the video episodes are used to illustrate grammatical structures in both presentation and practice.

Students at various proficiency levels can benefit from using the *Grammar Guides*. Lower-level students will find the *Grammar Guides* a valuable resource tool they can rely on to help them internalize the authentic language of the video. More advanced students will welcome the carefully sequenced review of the language and its connection to the video through numerous examples and practices.

LANGUAGE SKILLS

Grammar Guides 1-4 provide practice with the linguistic building blocks of the language. They give students an opportunity to analyze and review the structures through clear and simple grammar charts and explanations. Exercises are transparent and help students build from a receptive understanding of the grammar point to language production through controlled exercises and finally, free-writing, using the grammar point to talk about their own lives. The grammar charts and explanations are particularly helpful to students whose learning style relies on analysis and explanation. The opportunities for practice are useful to students who learn language inductively through observation and practice with the structures.

OPTIONS FOR USE

Each *Grammar Guide* can be used in a variety of different learning environments, including classroom, distance learning, tutorial, and/or independent study situations. Students can use *Grammar Guides 1-4* before or after they watch the corresponding video episode, to either preview or review critical structures and grammatical topics.

Grammar Guides 1-4 can easily be combined with other corresponding texts in the **Connect with English** print program. For classes with an emphasis on listening, *Video Comprehension Books 1-4* help students build listening comprehension skills and gain a clear understanding of the characters and story line in the video series. For classes with an emphasis on oral communication skills, *Conversation Books 1-4* contain a variety of pair, group, team,and whole-class activities based on important themes and events from each episode. Finally, there are 16 *Connections Readers* that offer students graded reading practice based on the **Connect with English** story. These readers also use the same grammatical scope and sequence found in *Grammar Guides 1-4.*

A VISUAL TOUR of this Text

This visual tour is designed to introduce the key features of *Grammar Guide 3*. The primary focus of each *Grammar Guide* is to help students develop mastery of key grammatical structures and concepts. *Grammar Guide 3* corresponds to episodes 25-36 of **Connect with English**. The scope and sequence of the grammar points in this book are developmental; topics become more advanced as the chapters progress.

Grammar Charts
The **Grammar Chart** explains the grammar topic and acts as a model that students can refer to as they do the exercises.

Photos
Photos from the corresponding video episode are used to illustrate the meaning of the grammar point.

Notes
The **Notes** section offers additional explanations about the material being presented. These sections have been carefully worded so that the language of instruction is no more advanced than the grammatical structures being presented in the text.

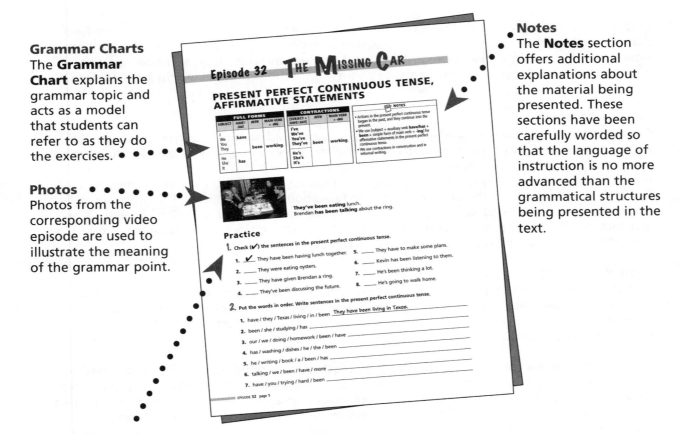

Contextualized Exercises
The first exercise in the **Practice** section is always based on the characters, situations, and events that happen in the video. This first exercise is also usually on the receptive level, allowing students to recognize the structural point before they actually need to produce it.

Chapter Structure

Every episode of *Grammar Guide 3* presents three grammar points, each on a two-page spread. Each grammar presentation has the following features:

• A grammar chart, illustrating the structures or grammatical features;

• Simple explanatory usage notes;

• A photo from the video episode illustrating the context of the grammar point;

• A practice section of exercises taking the student from a receptive knowledge to productive practice with the structure;

• A more advanced practice (**Power Practice**) section providing the student with an opportunity for free writing about his/her own life using the target structure.

Guided Practice

Subsequent exercises in the **Practice** section provide students with an opportunity to further practice the structure. The task in each exercise increases slightly in difficulty throughout each lesson. Some of these exercises are focused on the video, and others are set in other real-world contexts. The language used in all exercises — in direction lines, examples, and the items themselves — is very simple and utilizes only the structures that have been introduced up to that point in the book.

Relating Grammar to Everyday Life
The **Power Practice** section allows a chance for students to use the target structure to write about things that are meaningful in their own lives. It's a particularly useful tool for multilevel classrooms, as it gives students an opportunity to produce language at a variety of different levels.

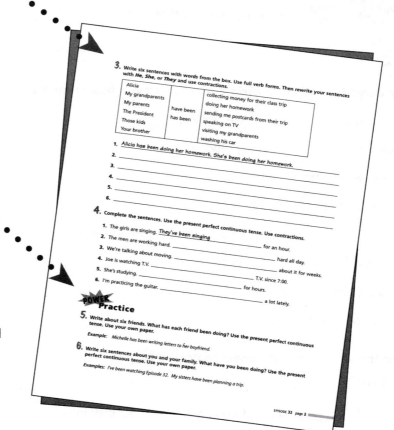

REBECCA REMEMBERS

USED TO: AFFIRMATIVE AND NEGATIVE STATEMENTS

AFFIRMATIVE STATEMENTS

SUBJECT	*USED TO*	MAIN VERB	
I We You They He She It	used to	**work**	at night.
		run	every day.
		be	fast.

NEGATIVE STATEMENTS

SUBJECT	*DID + NOT*	*USE TO*	MAIN VERB	
I We You They He She It	did not didn't	use to	**work**	at night.
			run	every day.
			be	fast.

 NOTES
- We use [**used to** + simple form of main verb] for habits or situations in the past that do not exist in the present.
- We use [**did not** + **use to** + simple form of main verb] for negative statements.
- **Did** is the *auxiliary verb* in negative statements with **use to**. We use auxiliary verbs in combination with main verbs.
- We can also use **did** alone as a main verb: *He did his homework.*

Rebecca **used to live** in Boston.

Practice

1. Underline *used to*, and circle *didn't use to*. Draw a box around the main verb.

1. The Mendoza family used to [live] in Mexico.

2. Rebecca (didn't use to) [feel] so guilty.

3. Mr. Casey used to be a fireman.

4. Kevin didn't use to study a lot in school.

5. Mr. Casey and Rebecca used to worry about Kevin's exams.

6. Rebecca and Sandy used to work together.

7. Matt used to be Rebecca's boyfriend in Boston.

8. Rebecca's life didn't use to be so complicated.

2. Complete the sentences with *used to* or *use to*.

1. I __used to__ drive fast.

2. You _____ write letters often.

3. We didn't _____ fight.

4. They _____ ski every winter.

5. It didn't _____ be so difficult.

6. She _____ be my girlfriend.

3. Rewrite the affirmative sentences below with *used to*. Rewrite the negative sentences with *didn't* + *use to*.

1. Julio goes to parties every night. _Julio used to go to parties every night._

2. The house isn't clean. _The house didn't use to be clean._

3. They are married. _____

4. We don't eat at expensive restaurants. _____

5. I see my grandparents on the weekends. _____

6. Serge runs very fast. _____

7. Doris reads a lot. _____

POWER Practice

4. Write about your childhood. Write six sentences about things you used to do as a child.

Example: *I used to drink a lot of milk.*

1. _____

2. _____

3. _____

4. _____

5. _____

6. _____

5. Write six sentences about things you *didn't* use to do as a child. Use *didn't* + *use to* in each sentence.

Example: *I didn't use to eat spinach.*

1. _____

2. _____

3. _____

4. _____

5. _____

6. _____

DRAWING CONCLUSIONS: *MIGHT* AND *MUST* IN AFFIRMATIVE AND NEGATIVE STATEMENTS

	SUBJECT	MIGHT / MUST		MAIN VERB	
AFFIRMATIVE STATEMENTS	Mr. Casey	might		need	an operation.
	Rebecca and Kevin	must		be	upset
	SUBJECT	**MIGHT / MUST**	**NOT**	**MAIN VERB**	
NEGATIVE STATEMENTS	Rebecca	might	not	return	to San Francisco.
	Rebecca and Kevin	must		feel	very happy.

NOTES

- We use **might** for a *weak* prediction or conclusion in the present or future. It is possible.
- We use **must** for a *strong* prediction or conclusion in the present. It is probable.
- **Might** and **must** are auxiliary verbs.

Mrs. Wang **must** like Rebecca.

Practice

6. Write **W** for sentences with weak prediction. Write **S** for sentences with strong prediction. Write **N** for sentences with no prediction.

1. __W__ Mr. Casey might not get better.

2. __S__ His condition must be serious.

3. __N__ He is in the hospital.

4. _____ Kevin is alone with his sick father.

5. _____ He must want Rebecca's help.

6. _____ Rebecca must feel guilty.

7. _____ Ramón might be in love with Rebecca.

8. _____ He must be worried about her.

7. Match each sentence on the left with a conclusion on the right.

1. __c__ Luis got an "A" on the test.

2. _____ Emily did not finish her dinner.

3. _____ Carlos is not at work.

4. _____ The team is very good.

5. _____ You bought a sports car.

6. _____ Tom and Mary had an argument.

a. It might win the game.

b. You must like to drive fast.

✔**c.** He must be happy.

d. They might not get married.

e. She must not be hungry.

f. He might be at home.

8. Put the words below in the correct order. Write sentences.

1. have / he / enough / must / money / not   <u>He must not have enough money.</u>

2. be / answer / might / his / correct / not   _____

3. tired / she / be / must   _____

4. hotel / the / close / beach / must / the / to / be   _____

5. food / we / need / more / might   _____

9. Change the following affirmative statements to negative.

1. We might get a new car.   <u>We might not get a new car.</u>

2. She might win the lottery.   _____

3. They must be the new students.   _____

4. He must live in Japan.   _____

POWER Practice

10. What might you do next year? Write five predictions about your life. Use *might*.

Examples: I might go to Brazil.   I might go on a diet.

1. _____
2. _____
3. _____
4. _____
5. _____

11. Write five statements about your friends or classmates. Then write five predictions or conclusions about them. Use *might* or *must*.

Examples: Lee is homesick.   He might go home next year.
                Paulo gets good grades.   He must study a lot.

1. _____
2. _____
3. _____
4. _____
5. _____

CARDINAL AND ORDINAL NUMBERS

CARDINAL NUMBERS		
1	one	
2	two	
3	three	
4	four	
5	five	
6	six	
7	seven	
8	eight	
9	nine	
10	ten	
11	eleven	
12	twelve	
13	thirteen	
14	fourteen	
15	fifteen	
16	sixteen	
17	seventeen	
18	eighteen	
19	nineteen	
20	twenty	
21	twenty-one	
22	twenty-two	
30	thirty	
40	forty	
50	fifty	
60	sixty	
70	seventy	
80	eighty	
90	ninety	
100	a hundred (or) one hundred	

ORDINAL NUMBERS		
1st	first	
2nd	second	
3rd	third	
4th	fourth	
5th	fifth	
6th	sixth	
7th	seventh	
8th	eighth	
9th	ninth	
10th	tenth	
11th	eleventh	
12th	twelfth	
13th	thirteenth	
14th	fourteenth	
15th	fifteenth	
16th	sixteenth	
17th	seventeenth	
18th	eighteenth	
19th	nineteenth	
20th	twentieth	
21st	twenty-first	
22nd	twenty-second	
30th	thirtieth	
40th	fortieth	
50th	fiftieth	
60th	sixtieth	
70th	seventieth	
80th	eightieth	
90th	ninetieth	
100th	one hundredth	

NOTES

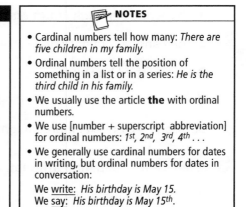

- Cardinal numbers tell how many: *There are five children in my family.*
- Ordinal numbers tell the position of something in a list or in a series: *He is the third child in his family.*
- We usually use the article **the** with ordinal numbers.
- We use [number + superscript abbreviation] for ordinal numbers: 1st, 2nd, 3rd, 4th . . .
- We generally use cardinal numbers for dates in writing, but ordinal numbers for dates in conversation:
  We <u>write</u>: *His birthday is May 15.*
  We <u>say</u>: *His birthday is May 15th.*

Kevin is the **second** child in the Casey family.

Practice

12. Underline the cardinal numbers. Circle the ordinal numbers.

Next month, Rebecca will have <u>four</u> final exams. It is the (third) month of the semester at the San Francisco College of Music. But Rebecca has to leave San Francisco for the first time. She has to see her sick father in Boston. She is now sitting in the twentieth row of an airplane. There are about one hundred people on the plane. The plane ticket to Boston cost five hundred dollars. The plane ride takes almost six hours. It is a very long flight. Rebecca will see her father in two more hours. He is on the third floor of the hospital in Boston.

13. Complete the sentences. Circle the answers.

1. We had ___five___ tests this semester.
    a. fifth   (**b.** five)

2. The _____ test was the hardest.
    a. fourth   **b.** four

3. I read _____ books this semester.
    a. seven   **b.** seventh

4. The _____ book was my favorite.
    a. two   **b.** second

5. The building has _____ floors.
    a. thirteen   **b.** thirteenth

6. Her office is on the _____ floor.
    a. seven   **b.** seventh

14. Complete the sentences with cardinal or ordinal numbers. Write the numbers as words.

1. I eat _three_____ meals each day.

2. I have _____ brothers and sisters.

3. I am the _____ child in my family.

4. This is the _____ exercise in this episode.

5. This is the _____ episode in *Connect With English*.

6. There are _____ days in this month.

7. Today is the _____ day of the month.

15. Look at Rosa's class schedule for Mondays. Complete the sentences. Use cardinal and ordinal numbers.

9:00 – 9:50	English 100
10:00 – 10:50	Sociology 101
11:00 – 11:50	Math 103
LUNCH	
2:00 – 4:50	Biology 100 – Lab

1. Rosa has _three classes_____ in the morning.

2. She has _____ in the afternoon.

3. Her _____ is English.

4. _____ is Sociology.

5. _____ is Math.

6. She spends _____ hours at school.

POWER Practice

16. Write five sentences about you and your family. Use cardinal or ordinal numbers. Use your own paper.

Examples: *My birthday is August 15.*
My sister Ellen is the third child.

17. Write five sentences about your city, town, or county. Use cardinal or ordinal numbers. Use your own paper.

Examples: *The first library in my city opened in 1960.*
There are four museums in my city.

THE EMERGENCY

PAST CONTINUOUS TENSE, AFFIRMATIVE STATEMENTS

SUBJECT	WAS / WERE	MAIN VERB + -ING	
I He She It	**was**	**making**	a lot of noise.
We You They	**were**	**sleeping**	late yesterday.

📝 **NOTES**

- We use the past continuous tense for actions in progress in the past.
- We use [subject + auxiliary verb **was** / **were** + simple form of main verb + **-ing**] for affirmative statements in the past continuous tense.
- We use **was** and **were** as the auxiliary verbs in the past continuous tense. We can also use **was** or **were** alone as main verbs in the simple past tense: *He was here. They were students.*

Kevin **was waiting** for Rebecca at the airport.

Practice

1. Check (✔) the sentences in the past continuous tense.

1. ✔ Mr. Casey was holding his chest.

2. _____ Kevin called for help.

3. _____ The ambulance driver was asking questions.

4. _____ Kevin was answering the questions.

5. _____ The ambulance arrived in five minutes.

6. _____ The doctors were taking care of Mr. Casey.

7. _____ Rebecca and Kevin were arguing at home.

8. _____ The phone rang.

2. Complete the sentences with *was* or *were*.

1. He _____was_____ writing a letter.

2. The students _____ studying.

3. I _____ resting in my room.

4. We _____ thinking about the movie.

5. The mechanic _____ taking a break.

6. The birds _____ singing.

7. The secretary _____ complaining.

8. They _____ traveling all month.

9. She _____ cooking for hours.

10. The computer _____ flashing.

3. Rewrite the sentences below in the past continuous tense.

1. He went to the store.   He was going to the store.

2. They cleaned the kitchen.   _____

3. We worked very hard.   _____

4. She thought about her family.   _____

5. I ate a hamburger.   _____

6. The truck moved fast.   _____

7. Eva and Claude did their homework.   _____

POWER Practice

4. Think of the last time you were with your family. What were you and your family members doing? Write six sentences with the past continuous tense.

Example: *My father and brother were watching a soccer game on TV.*

1. _____

2. _____

3. _____

4. _____

5. _____

6. _____

5. What were you doing a year ago? Write six sentences with the past continuous tense.

Example: *I was taking an art class.*

1. _____

2. _____

3. _____

4. _____

5. _____

6. _____

PAST CONTINUOUS TENSE, NEGATIVE STATEMENTS

FULL FORMS			
SUBJECT	**WAS / WERE**	**NOT**	**MAIN VERB + -ING**
I He She It	**was**	**not**	**listening**.
We You They	**were**		

CONTRACTIONS		
SUBJECT	**[WAS / WERE + NOT]**	**MAIN VERB + -ING**
I He She It	**wasn't**	**listening**.
We You They	**weren't**	

📝 NOTES

- We use [subject + auxiliary verb **was/were** + **not** + simple form of main verb + **-ing**] for negative statements in the past continuous tense.
- We use contractions in conversation and in informal writing.

Mr. Casey **wasn't breathing** normally.

Practice

6. Underline the sentences with the negative past continuous tense.

Rebecca and Kevin were very worried about their father. <u>He wasn't doing well</u>. His heart wasn't beating strongly. He wasn't talking. He was still and quiet. The doctors explained his condition. They were not considering surgery. Mr. Casey was too weak. The doctors weren't planning to do anything for 48 hours. They were watching him carefully.

7. Change the full forms to contractions. Write the correct verb forms in the spaces.

1. I was not thinking about him.　　　　　I _wasn't thinking_ about him.

2. We were not enjoying the movie.　　　We _____ the movie.

3. He was not eating the food.　　　　　He _____ the food.

4. They were not paying their bills.　　　They _____ their bills.

5. The car was not working.　　　　　　The car _____.

6. She was not driving fast.　　　　　　She _____ fast.

8. Complete the sentences with negative past continuous tense verb forms. Use contractions.

1. (sit)   I _wasn't sitting_ with my friend.

2. (lose)   I _____ the game.

3. (listen)   The students _____ to the teacher.

4. (help)   Paulo _____ his wife.

5. (work)   The plan _____.

6. (play)   The musicians _____ well.

7. (meet)   We _____ any interesting people.

9. PRETEND: Someone is accusing you of the actions below. You didn't do these things. Write six sentences with the negative past continuous tense. Use full forms for extra emphasis.

1. You were cheating on the exam.   _I was not cheating on the exam._

2. You were sleeping on the job.   _____

3. You were hitting your sister.   _____

4. You were reading my diary.   _____

5. You were driving too fast.   _____

6. You were lying about your age.   _____

POWER Practice

10. How was your life different ten years ago? Write ten sentences with the negative past continuous tense. Use your own paper.

Examples: *I wasn't driving a car ten years ago.   I wasn't studying English ten years ago.*

11. How were your parents' lives different 20 years ago? Write ten sentences with the negative past continuous tense. Use your own paper.

Examples: *They weren't taking vacations 20 years ago.   My parents weren't using a computer 20 years ago.*

STATIVE VERBS

SUBJECT	STATIVE VERB	
I	see	the plane.
We	know	his name.
You	want	a lot.
They	seemed	nice.
He	loves	the food.
She	was	beautiful.
It	smells	good.

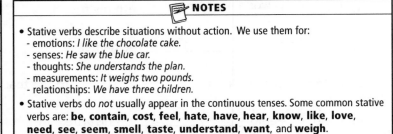

NOTES

- Stative verbs describe situations without action. We use them for:
  - emotions: *I like the chocolate cake.*
  - senses: *He saw the blue car.*
  - thoughts: *She understands the plan.*
  - measurements: *It weighs two pounds.*
  - relationships: *We have three children.*
- Stative verbs do *not* usually appear in the continuous tenses. Some common stative verbs are: **be, contain, cost, feel, hate, have, hear, know, like, love, need, see, seem, smell, taste, understand, want,** and **weigh.**

Rebecca **seems** angry. The apartment **is** a mess.

Practice

12. Check (✔) the sentences with stative verbs.

1. ✔ Mr. Casey's condition is very serious.

2. _____ Kevin was trying to help his father.

3. _____ Dr. Lincoln and Rebecca were discussing the situation.

4. _____ Rebecca understood the doctor's explanation.

5. _____ She wants a second opinion.

6. _____ Rebecca and Kevin were arguing about family responsibilities.

7. _____ Rebecca didn't know about her father's eating habits.

8. _____ Rebecca and Kevin are going back to the hospital.

13. Circle the correct form of the stative verbs in the sentences below.

Dear Anne,

Everything (is)/ is being fine here. I have / am having three more exams at school. This semester seems / is seeming very hard. Yesterday I had / was having my math exam. I hate / am hating math. But I knew / was knowing most of the answers. The test contained / was containing twenty questions. Good luck with your exams!

Love,

Gabriela

14. Write ten sentences with words from each box. Write five sentences in the simple present tense and five sentences in the simple past tense.

I	The book	taste	be	expensive	long
My friend	The necklace	feel	have	fantastic	interesting
You	The building	weigh	love	a lot	chocolate
My teacher	The French fries	hate	want	money	ice cream
My parents	His dogs	cost	smell	terrible	a handsome boyfriend

1. My friend loves chocolate. _____

2. _____

3. _____

4. _____

5. _____

6. _____

7. _____

8. _____

9. _____

10. _____

POWER Practice

15. Write five compliments to your mother. Use stative verbs.

Examples: You look great.   I love your sweater.

1. _____

2. _____

3. _____

4. _____

5. _____

16. What bothers you? Write five complaints with stative verbs. Use your own paper.

Examples: I hate to wait a long time for a bus.   Gasoline smells awful.

PAST CONTINUOUS TENSE, *YES/NO* QUESTIONS AND SHORT ANSWERS

YES / NO QUESTIONS			AFFIRMATIVE SHORT ANSWERS			NEGATIVE SHORT ANSWERS		
WAS / WERE	SUBJECT	MAIN VERB + -ING	YES	SUBJECT	WAS / WERE	NO	SUBJECT	WAS / WERE + NOT
Was	I he she it		Yes,	I he she it	was.	No,	I he she it	was not. wasn't.
Were	we you they	sleeping?		we you they	were.		we you they	were not. weren't.

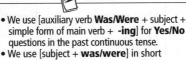

NOTES

- We use [auxiliary verb **Was/Were** + subject + simple form of main verb + **-ing**] for **Yes/No** questions in the past continuous tense.
- We use [subject + **was/were**] in short answers with **Yes** in the past continuous tense. These are like short answers with **BE** in the past tense.
- We use [subject + **was/were** + **not**] in short answers with **No** in the past continuous tense. These are like short answers with **BE** in the past tense.

Was Sandy **telling** the truth?

Practice

1. Check (✔) the *Yes/No* questions in the past continuous tense.

1. ✔ Was Mr. Casey living with Kevin?
2. _____ Father O'Connor was helping Kevin and Rebecca.
3. _____ Was Father O'Connor praying for Mr. Casey?
4. _____ Are Kevin and Rebecca acting calmly?
5. _____ Did Mr. Casey ask for his brother?
6. _____ Were Rebecca and Sandy talking about Jack?

2. Complete the questions with *Was* or *Were*. Complete the answers with *was, were, wasn't,* or *weren't*.

1. _Was_____ the television working?

   Yes, it _was_____.

2. _____ your father yelling?

   No, he _____.

3. _____ his sisters crying?

   Yes, they _____.

4. _____ we playing too loudly?

   No, you _____.

3. What were you doing when you were 10 years old? Answer the questions with short answers. Use contractions.

1. Were you driving a car? _____No, I wasn't._____

2. Were you going to school? _____

3. Were you taking care of your brothers or sisters? _____

4. Were you working? _____

5. Were you learning English? _____

6. Were you playing sports? _____

4. Complete the questions. Use the verb in parentheses. Use the past continuous tense.

1. (smile) ___Was he smiling___ for the picture?　　Yes, he was.

2. (talk) _____ on the phone?　　No, she wasn't.

3. (say) _____ the word correctly?　　Yes, we were.

4. (make) _____ too much noise?　　Yes, it was.

5. (wear) _____ their new clothes?　　No, they weren't.

6. (bother) _____ you?　　Yes, you were.

POWER Practice

5. Write five *Yes/No* questions about your friends. Use the past continuous tense.

Examples: *Was Pedro sleeping in class yesterday?*
Were Noriko and Keiko studying last night?

1. _____

2. _____

3. _____

4. _____

5. _____

6. PRETEND: You went away on vacation. Your two teenaged children stayed at home. You returned, and the house looked terrible. Ask your children about their activities. Write five *Yes/No* questions with the past continuous tense. Use your own paper.

Example: *Were you playing soccer in the living room?*

PAST CONTINUOUS TENSE, *WH-* QUESTIONS

WH- QUESTION WORD	WAS / WERE	SUBJECT	MAIN VERB + -ING
Who Whom	was	he	**teaching**?
What	was	she	**reading**?
When	were	we	**talking**?
Where	were	they	**going**?

📝 **NOTES**

- We use [**Wh-** question word + auxiliary verb **was/were** + subject + simple form of main verb + **-ing**] for information questions in the past continuous tense.
- The subject comes between **was/were** and the main verb.
- We use **Who** in conversation and in informal writing. We use **Whom** in formal writing and in formal speaking.

Rebecca: ***What were* you *saying*?**

Practice

7. Circle the correct word.

1. (What) / When was the doctor saying?

2. Who / Where were Kevin and Rebecca sleeping?

3. Where / Who was Rebecca calling?

4. What / When were Kevin and Rebecca arguing?

5. Where / What were Brendan and Anne living?

6. What / Who was Brendan doing?

7. Who / When was Brendan arriving?

8. When / Who were Father O'Connor and Rebecca talking about?

8. Match the questions and answers.

1. __c__ Who was he helping?

2. _____ What were you writing?

3. _____ When were they playing in Germany?

4. _____ Where was she going?

5. _____ What was he looking for?

6. _____ Where were our parents sitting?

a. To the bank.

b. In the front row.

✔c. My son.

d. A letter.

e. Two years ago.

f. His keys.

9. Put the words in the correct order. Write *Wh-* questions.

1. living / Korea / when / she / was / in   When was she living in Korea? _____

2. you / painting / were / what   _____

3. was / it / who / helping   _____

4. flowers / where / the / growing / were   _____

5. the / saying / was / what / president   _____

6. were / where / they / class / the / taking   _____

7. taking / was / to / who / dinner / he   _____

10. Write a question for each answer. Use the past continuous tense.

Example: *What were you making?*   *A chocolate cake.*

Questions: **Answers:**

1. _____   My father.

2. _____   At the library.

3. _____   Last year.

4. _____   To the airport.

5. _____   A book.

POWER Practice

11. Interview a friend, classmate, or neighbor. Write five *Wh-* questions for him/her. Use the past continuous tense.

Examples: *What English class were you taking last semester?*   *Where was Alicia going yesterday?*

1. _____

2. _____

3. _____

4. _____

5. _____

12. Ask a friend or family member about a specific one-year time period in his/her life. Write *Wh-* questions. Use the past continuous tense. Use your own paper.

Example: *What were you and Mother doing in 1992?*

THERE IS/ARE AND *THERE WAS/WERE:* YES/NO QUESTIONS AND SHORT ANSWERS

YES/NO QUESTIONS			
IS/WAS	THERE	SINGULAR SUBJECT	
Is Was	there	a telephone	in your room?
ARE/WERE	THERE	PLURAL SUBJECT	
Are Were	there	restaurants	in the mall?

AFFIRMATIVE SHORT ANSWERS		
YES,	THERE	IS/WAS
Yes,	there	is. was.
YES,	THERE	ARE/WERE
Yes,	there	are. were.

NEGATIVE SHORT ANSWERS		
NO,	THERE	IS/WAS + NOT
No,	there	is not. isn't. was not. wasn't.
NO,	THERE	ARE/WERE + NOT
No,	there	are not. aren't. were not. weren't.

NOTES
- We use [**BE** + **there** + subject] for **Yes/No** questions in the simple present tense and in the simple past tense.
- We use [**there** + **BE**] in short answers with **Yes**.
- We use [**there** + **BE** + **not**] in short answers with **No**.

Are there comfortable chairs in the hospital?

Is there a visitor for Rebecca?

Practice

13. Check (✔) the *Yes/No* questions with *Is/Are there* and *Was/Were there*.

1. ✔ Was there good news about Mr. Casey?

2. _____ There are nurses in Mr. Casey's hospital room.

3. _____ Is there a phone on Brendan Casey's farm?

4. _____ Were Brendan and Anne Casey at home?

5. _____ Are there cows on Brendan's farm?

6. _____ There wasn't any food in the Caseys' refrigerator.

7. _____ Was there a cafeteria in the hospital?

8. _____ Were there bruises on Sandy's face?

14. Complete the questions with *Is there* or *Are there*.

1. __Is there__ anything interesting on the TV?

2. _____ a lot of students in your class?

3. _____ anything cheap on the menu?

4. _____ a doctor here?

5. _____ any clean towels?

6. _____ a phone nearby?

15. Complete the questions with *Was there* or *Were there*.

1. <u>Was there</u> much traffic this morning?

2. _____ many famous paintings in the museum?

3. _____ a good sale at the store?

4. _____ enough people on the team?

5. _____ a car in the driveway?

16. Answer the questions about the schedule below. Use short answers.

This Semester's Class Schedule				
Monday	Tuesday	Wednesday	Thursday	Friday
geometry	history	geometry	history	speech
algebra	economics	computer science	economics	algebra
physics	Russian	women's studies	Russian	physics

Last Semester's Class Schedule				
Monday	Tuesday	Wednesday	Thursday	Friday
English	French	English	French	art
calculus	Spanish	music	Spanish	music
history	Japanese	art	Japanese	history

This Semester

1. Are there math classes on Monday? <u>Yes, there are.</u>

2. Is there an art class on Tuesday and Thursday? _____

3. Are there computer classes on Monday and Friday? _____

4. Is there a women's studies class on Wednesday? _____

Last Semester

5. Was there a music class on Wednesday? _____

6. Were there language classes on Tuesday and Thursday? _____

7. Was there a music class on Monday? _____

8. Were there science classes on Friday? _____

POWER Practice

17. PRETEND: You are moving to a new city. Write ten questions about this new city. Use *Is there* and *Are there*. Use your own paper.

Example: Are there discos in Hong Kong?

18. Ask your friends or family members about their childhood homes. Write five *Yes/No* questions with *Was there* and *Were there*. Use your own paper.

Examples: Were there pictures on the walls? Was there a park in your neighborhood?

ADVERBIAL PHRASES AND CLAUSES: ONE ACTION BEFORE OR AFTER ANOTHER ACTION

MAIN CLAUSE	ADVERBIAL PHRASE
We had dinner	after the game.
	ADVERBIAL CLAUSE
	after we watched the game.

ADVERBIAL PHRASE	MAIN CLAUSE
After the game,	we had dinner.
ADVERBIAL CLAUSE	
After we watched the game,	

📝 NOTES

- A phrase is a group of words without [subject + verb].
- A clause is a group of words with [subject + verb].
- A sentence with an adverbial phrase or clause can show one action *before* or *after* another. We can use **before**, **after**, or **when**. We use **when** in clauses only.
- We can use **when** to mean *immediately after*: *When I heard the news, I left the party.*
- An adverbial phrase or clause can come *before* or *after* the main clause of the sentence.
- We use a comma after an adverbial phrase or clause at the beginning of a sentence.

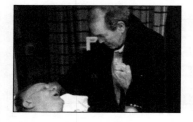

When the two brothers saw each other,
they made their peace.

Practice

1. Underline the adverbial clauses. Circle the adverbial phrases.

Brendan meets Rebecca and Kevin <u>before he sees Patrick.</u> After a short talk with them, he goes in to see his brother alone. Patrick opens his eyes when he hears Brendan. When Patrick can speak, he tells his brother, "I'm glad you came." After these words, Brendan says he's ready to forgive and forget. When he hears this, Patrick offers his hand, and Brendan takes it. They make their peace before Patrick dies.

2. Write *1* next to the action that happens first and *2* next to the action that happens afterward.

1. __2__ Before work, __1__ we got some coffee.

2. _____ After I finished my book, _____ I went to bed.

3. _____ After he fixes it, _____ the car will run better.

4. _____ When she saw me, _____ she started to laugh.

5. _____ I'll call you _____ when I get home.

3. Rewrite the sentences with the adverbial clause or phrase at the beginning. Use commas.

1. We went inside when the rain started. <u>When the rain started, we went inside.</u>

2. He took a break after he studied for two hours. _____

3. Please tell me before you leave. _____

4. They ate in a restaurant before the concert. _____

5. I'll make dinner after I finish this letter. _____

6. We were surprised when she began to cry. _____

4. Combine the two sentences in two ways. Use adverbial clauses. Use commas when you need them.

1. *First:* I had breakfast. *Next:* I brushed my teeth.

   a. After <u>I had breakfast, I brushed my teeth.</u>

   b. <u>I brushed my teeth</u>　after　<u>I had breakfast.</u>

2. *First:* She said good-bye. *Next:* She boarded the plane.

   a. _____ before _____

   b. Before _____

3. *First:* It started to rain. *Next:* We opened our umbrellas.

   a. When _____

   b. _____ when _____

4. *First:* We do our homework. *Next:* We watch TV.

   a. After _____

   b. _____ after _____

POWER Practice

5. Write six sentences with adverbial clauses about your usual morning routine. Use the simple present tense and *before*, *after*, or *when*. Use your own paper.

Examples: *I wake up when I hear my alarm.   After I get dressed, I make breakfast.*

6. What did you do yesterday evening? Write six sentences with adverbial phrases or clauses about your activities. Use the simple past tense. Use your own paper.

Examples: *When I got home, I had dinner.   After dinner, I washed the dishes.*

ADVERBIAL PHRASES AND CLAUSES: TWO ACTIONS AT THE SAME TIME

MAIN CLAUSE	ADVERBIAL PHRASE
She was sewing	during the game.
	ADVERBIAL CLAUSE
	while she was watching the game.

ADVERBIAL PHRASE	MAIN CLAUSE
During dinner,	we were talking about the game.
ADVERBIAL CLAUSE	
While we were having dinner,	

NOTES

- A sentence with an adverbial phrase or clause can show two actions or situations *at the same time.*
- We can use [**during** + noun phrase] in an adverbial phrase.
- We can use [**while** or **when** + subject + verb] in an adverbial clause.
- The adverbial phrase or clause can come *before* or *after* the main clause.
- We use a comma after an adverbial phrase or clause at the beginning of a sentence.

While Brendan was talking to Patrick,
Rebecca was looking for Sandy.

Practice

7. Check (✔) the sentences with two actions or situations at the same time.

1. ___✔___ While Brendan was visiting Patrick, Rebecca was returning to the cafeteria.

2. _____ While Rebecca was looking for Sandy, Kevin was waiting in the hall.

3. _____ Sandy left before Rebecca got back to the cafeteria.

4. _____ Kevin was getting a drink while he and Rebecca were talking.

5. _____ After Rebecca told Kevin about Sandy, he got angry at Jack.

6. _____ Brendan was talking with Patrick during this time.

8. Circle *when, while,* or *during.*

1. Rebecca and Kevin were waiting outside (when)/ during Brendan was visiting Patrick.

2. While / During the doctors were trying to save Patrick, his children were watching.

3. Patrick's heart wasn't beating when / during this time.

4. Brendan was holding Rebecca while / during she was crying.

5. While / During his phone call home, Brendan was speaking quietly.

9. Combine the two sentences. Use an adverbial phrase with *during*.

1. I was reading. I was having breakfast. I was reading during breakfast.

2. She was eating popcorn. She was watching the movie. _____

3. We were cheering. The game was going on. _____

4. I was watching TV. They were having an argument. _____

5. I was listening closely. I was having an interview. _____

10. Rewrite each sentence with an adverbial clause. Use *while* + the past continuous tense of the verb in parentheses.

1. During my trip to New York, I was listening to the radio. (drive)

   While I was driving to New York, I was listening to the radio.

2. During the baseball game, they were eating hot dogs. (watch)

   _____

3. During dinner, we were talking about the news. (eat)

   _____

4. During the concert, I was thinking about you. (listen)

   _____

5. During the wait for his doctor, he was looking at a magazine. (wait)

   _____

POWER Practice

11. Complete the sentences. Use the past continuous tense.

Example: During dinner last night, I was watching the news.

1. During dinner last night, I _____

2. While I was studying, _____

3. I was eating _____ while _____

4. When I was sleeping, _____

5. During lunch yesterday, _____

12. Write six sentences about you and your friends or family. Write adverbial clauses with *while*. Use the past continuous tense. Use your own paper.

Example: While I was doing my homework, my roommate was talking on the phone.

PAST CONTINUOUS TENSE AND SIMPLE PAST TENSE

PAST CONTINUOUS TENSE	
I **was taking** a shower	while he **was making** lunch.
SIMPLE PAST TENSE	
I **took** a shower,	and we **had** lunch.
PAST CONTINUOUS TENSE	**SIMPLE PAST TENSE**
While I **was taking** a shower,	the phone **rang**.
I **was taking** a shower	when the phone **rang**.

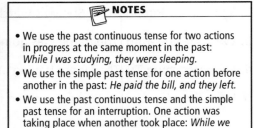

NOTES

- We use the past continuous tense for two actions in progress at the same moment in the past: *While I was studying, they were sleeping.*
- We use the simple past tense for one action before another in the past: *He paid the bill, and they left.*
- We use the past continuous tense and the simple past tense for an interruption. One action was taking place when another took place: *While we were shopping, I met an old friend.*

While Rebecca **was talking** with Anne, she **asked** about Brendan's relationship with her father.

Practice

13. Check (✔) the sentences that show an interruption. These sentences have both the simple past tense and the past continuous tense.

1. __✔__ Alberto's flowers arrived while Rebecca and Kevin were talking.

2. _____ When Brendan arrived, he introduced his wife to Rebecca.

3. _____ While they were talking, Brendan was looking around for Kevin.

4. _____ While they were standing together, Kevin pointed out some people to Brendan.

5. _____ While Brendan and Kevin were talking, Brendan noticed Aunt Molly.

6. _____ When Rebecca asked Anne a question, the two women were sitting together.

14. Write *1* next to the action already taking place when another action took place.

1. ____ When the phone rang, __1__ we were watching a movie.

2. ____ My mother was making dinner ____ when I got home.

3. ____ While we were taking a walk, ____ the rain began.

4. ____ When you called, ____ I was studying.

5. ____ The fire started ____ while they were sleeping.

6. ____ He was moving a piano ____ when he hurt his back.

15. Circle the correct tense of the verb in these sentences about the story.

1. Rebecca lived / (was living) in San Francisco when her father had a heart attack.

2. Rebecca flew / was flying back to Boston when she heard the news.

3. Brendan came / was coming to Boston when he learned about Patrick's heart attack.

4. Patrick had his last heart attack while Brendan visited / was visiting with him.

5. Brendan telephoned his wife when Patrick died / was dying.

6. When Brendan and Kevin were talking at the funeral, Brendan saw / was seeing Aunt Molly.

16. Combine the two sentences. Use an adverbial clause with *while*, *when*, *before*, or *after*.

1. I was listening to a lecture. I fell asleep. _I fell asleep while I was listening to a lecture._

2. We were waiting for the bus. We were talking about you. _____

_____

3. He was skiing. He broke his leg. _____

4. They washed the car. They waxed it. _____

5. I was listening to the radio. I heard the news. _____

6. She was doing homework. She was eating a snack. _____

7. I thought about it carefully. I made my decision. _____

POWER Practice

17. Complete the following sentences about interruptions in your past. Use the simple past tense for the interruption.

Example: While I was taking a shower, somebody knocked on the door.

1. While I was eating dinner, _____

2. During dinner, _____

3. _____ while I was studying.

4. When I was sleeping, _____

5. During the night, _____

18. Write six sentences that show an interruption. Use the simple past tense with the past continuous tense. Use *when* or *while*. Write about you or your family or friends. Use your own paper.

Examples: I was sleeping when my alarm rang.   My brother got married while he was studying at the university.

INDIRECT OBJECT NOUNS AND PRONOUNS: AFFIRMATIVE AND NEGATIVE STATEMENTS

AFFIRMATIVE/NEGATIVE STATEMENTS—FORM 1		
	INDIRECT OBJECT NOUN/PRONOUN	DIRECT OBJECT NOUN
She gave She didn't give	**her brother** **Kevin** **him**	the book.

AFFIRMATIVE/NEGATIVE STATEMENTS—FORM 2			
	DIRECT OBJECT NOUN/PRONOUN	*TO*	INDIRECT OBJECT NOUN/PRONOUN
She gave She didn't give	the book it		**her brother**. **Kevin**. **him**.
		to	

📝 NOTES

- Some sentences have both a direct and an indirect object.
- The direct object answers the question **What:** *What did she give to Kevin? The book.* (**The book** = direct object.)
- The indirect object answers the question **Who. . . to** or **To whom:** *Who did she give the book to? Kevin.* or *To whom did she give the book? Kevin.* (**Kevin** = indirect object.)
- We can use [indirect object + direct object noun] after the main verb in a sentence: *Manuel sold Patricia the bicycle.*
- We can also use [direct object + to + indirect object] after the main verb in a sentence: *Manuel sold the bicycle to Patricia.*
- We often use indirect objects with the verbs **bring, give, hand, lend, pay, sell, send, show, tell,** and **write**.
- Indirect object pronouns have the same form as direct object pronouns: **me, us, you, them, him, her, it**.

The fire chief handed **Rebecca** a helmet.

The fire chief handed it **to her**.

Practice

1. Check (✔) the word order of the indirect objects and the direct objects in the sentences below.

	Form 1 [Indirect Object + Direct Object]	Form 2 [Direct Object + to + Indirect Object]
1. Kevin gave a rose to his father.	_____	✔
2. Kevin gave him a rose.	_____	_____
3. Rebecca didn't write her father a song.	_____	_____
4. Matt gave Rebecca a hug.	_____	_____
5. Rebecca didn't show Matt the helmet.	_____	_____
6. Rebecca didn't show it to him.	_____	_____
7. Jack didn't bring flowers to Rebecca.	_____	_____
8. Sandy didn't tell Rebecca her troubles.	_____	_____
9. Frank Wells offered his help to Rebecca and Kevin.	_____	_____

2. Change the indirect object nouns to indirect object pronouns.

1. (Walter) I paid _him_____ ten dollars.

2. (her sister) She didn't give the answers to _____.

3. (you and me) My father told _____ a story.

4. (the students) The teacher lends pens to _____ every day.

5. (the engineers) We sent _____ the equipment.

3. Rewrite the sentences. Change the order of the direct and indirect objects.

1. The man handed her the keys. _The man handed the keys to her._____

2. She told him a story. _____

3. He wrote his girlfriend a poem. _____

4. They sent their mother flowers. _____

5. You didn't tell them the truth. _____

4. Rewrite the sentences. Change the order of the direct and indirect objects.

1. Please pass the salt to me. _Please pass me the salt._____

2. You didn't show the photos to her. _____

3. The lawyer brought the papers to him. _____

4. Show the money to me. _____

5. They sold the computers to the students. _____

POWER Practice

5. Who did you give presents to last year? What presents did you give? Write five sentences with indirect object nouns and pronouns. Use your own paper.

Examples: *I gave my father a watch. I also gave him a tie.*

6. What did you lend people last year? Write five sentences with indirect object nouns and pronouns. Use your own paper.

Examples: *I lent my car to my sister. I also lent her some money.*

INDIRECT OBJECT NOUNS AND PRONOUNS: *YES/NO* QUESTIONS AND SHORT ANSWERS

YES/NO QUESTIONS—FORM 1		
	INDIRECT OBJECT NOUN/PRONOUN	**DIRECT OBJECT NOUN**
Did Rebecca give	her brother **Kevin** him	a hug?

YES/NO QUESTIONS—FORM 2			
	DIRECT OBJECT NOUN/PRONOUN	*TO*	**INDIRECT OBJECT NOUN/PRONOUN**
Did Rebecca give	a hug	to	her brother? **Kevin?** him?

SHORT ANSWERS
Yes, she did.
No, she didn't.

NOTES

- Some **Yes/No** questions have both a direct object and an indirect object.
- We can use [indirect object + direct object noun] after the main verb in **Yes/No** questions.
- We can also use [direct object + **to** + indirect object] after the main verb in **Yes/No** questions.

Does Rebecca give advice **to Sandy**?

Practice

1. Check (✔) the sentences with indirect objects. Then, underline the indirect object nouns or pronouns.

1. **✔** Does the fire chief give a helmet to <u>Rebecca and Kevin</u>?

2. _____ Does Frank Wells give a speech at the cemetery?

3. _____ Did Matt give Rebecca support?

4. _____ Did he tell her any lies?

5. _____ Could Matt stay a long time at the funeral home?

6. _____ Did Rebecca's friend bring Kevin a present?

7. _____ Did Jack bring flowers to Rebecca and Kevin?

8. _____ Did the priest say a prayer at the funeral?

9. _____ Did Rebecca tell Sandy her opinion of Jack?

10. _____ Did Sandy tell her problems to Rebecca?

11. _____ Did Rebecca show Sandy the helmet?

8. Change the sentences below to **Yes/No** questions. Change the indirect object nouns to pronouns.

1. Raul gave the players some water.

_Did Raul_____ give _them_____ some water?

2. She can show my husband and me the house.

_____ show _____ the house?

3. Rafael sells fruit to his customers.

_____ sell fruit to _____ ?

4. The citizens sent suggestions to the president.

_____ send suggestions to _____ ?

5. She could tell Robert the truth.

_____ tell _____ the truth?

9. Change the sentences to **Yes/No** questions. Change the order of the direct and indirect objects. Write short answers.

1. I write my parents letters.

Do you write letters to your parents? Yes, I do.

2. My brothers don't tell our parents the truth.

_____

3. The teacher gave Carlos a good grade.

_____

4. They can't sell things to people.

_____

5. They brought dinner to their friends.

_____

Practice

10. PRETEND: You are sitting at the dinner table with your family. Write five requests with **can** or **could**. Use indirect objects and direct objects. Use your own paper.

Examples: Could you pass me the butter? Can you hand the chicken to Lin?

INDIRECT OBJECTS AND DIRECT OBJECTS: *WH-* QUESTIONS AND ANSWERS

QUESTIONS WITH *WHO . . . TO*					
WHO	**AUX.**	**SUBJECT**	**MAIN VERB**	**DIRECT OBJECT**	**TO**
Who	did can will	she	give	**the money** **it**	**to**?

QUESTIONS WITH *TO WHOM*				
TO WHOM	**AUX.**	**SUBJECT**	**MAIN VERB**	**DIRECT OBJECT**
To whom	did can will	she	give	**the money**? **it**?

QUESTIONS WITH *WHAT*					
WHAT	**AUX.**	**SUBJECT**	**MAIN VERB**	**(TO)**	**INDIRECT OBJECT**
What	did can will	she	give	**(to)**	**her brother**? **him**?

ANSWERS

Her brother.
To her brother.
Him.
To him.

Her brother.
To her brother.
Him.
To him.

Some money.

📝 NOTES

- We use **Who . . . to** and **To whom** for questions about the indirect object.
- We use **To whom** only in formal writing and in formal speaking.
- We use **What** for questions about the direct object.
- In questions with **What**, the preposition **to** before the indirect object is optional:
  What did she give to him? = What did she give him?
- The abbreviation **AUX.** = auxiliary verb.
- We usually use auxiliary verbs in combination with main verbs in questions.
- We can use **do/does/did/will/can/could/should/may/might/must** as auxiliary verbs.

Who did people send flowers **to**?

Practice

11. **Write *F* for formal questions. Write *I* for informal questions.**

1. __F__ To whom do Rebecca and Kevin give roses?

2. _____ Who does Frank Wells offer his help to?

3. _____ To whom does Rebecca give a speech?

4. _____ Who does the fire chief give the helmet to?

5. _____ To whom can Rebecca tell her problems?

6. _____ Who can Kevin show his emotions to?

12. **Change the formal questions to informal questions.**

1. To whom did you show it? _Who did you show it to?_____

2. To whom can I tell my secret? _____

3. To whom will they donate the money? _____

4. To whom did she bring the food? _____

13. Complete the questions with *What*, *Who*, or *To whom*.

1. __What__ can she give to her parents?

2. _____ did they tell the story?

3. _____ do you give your wife for her birthday?

4. _____ could the students show their homework to?

5. _____ can I send the bill to?

14. Put the words in the correct order.

1. did / who / the / to / picture / you / show

   __Who did you show the picture to?__

2. boyfriend / to / give / Helga / what / her / did

   _____

3. who / secrets / tell / can / your / to / you

   _____

4. did / letter / write / whom / you / to / the

   _____

5. the / what / company / them / send / could

   _____

6. lend / to / table / who / did / you / the

   _____

POWER Practice

15. Answer the *Wh-* questions below with real answers about your life.

Example: Who do you tell your secrets to?   I tell my secrets to my sister.

1. Who do you tell your secrets to?

   _____

2. Who might you lend money to?

   _____

3. Who do you send letters to?

   _____

4. Who do you give advice to?

   _____

16. Write five *Wh-* questions with *Who...to* for a friend or family member. Write their answers. Use your own paper.

Examples: Who do you write letters to?
Who would you lend your car to?

LIFE GOES ON

PRESENT PERFECT TENSE, AFFIRMATIVE STATEMENTS

FULL FORMS			
SUBJECT	*HAVE / HAS*	**PAST PARTICIPLE**	
I We You They	**have**	**finished**	the work.
He She It	**has**		

CONTRACTIONS		
[SUBJECT + HAVE / HAS]	**PAST PARTICIPLE**	
I've We've You've They've	**finished**	the work.
He's She's It's		

📝 NOTES

- We use the present perfect tense for actions and situations that began in the past and continue into the present: *I have lived here since 1991.*
- We also use the present perfect tense for actions and situations that happened sometime in the past. We don't say when they happened: *She has visited us before.*
- We use [subject + auxiliary verb **have/has** + past participle of main verb] for present perfect tense statements.
- Regular past participles are [simple form of main verb + **-ed** or **-d**].
- We use contractions in conversation and in informal writing.

Rebecca: ***I've looked*** *at these cards.*

Brendan: *Can I look at them?*

Practice

1. Check (✔) the sentences in the present perfect tense.

1. **✔** Rebecca has looked at lots of cards.

2. _____ Some friends made a donation to the American Heart Association.

3. _____ Mrs. Peterson has cooked some food for Rebecca and Kevin.

4. _____ Brendan and Anne have talked about Kevin and Rebecca.

5. _____ Brendan's helped Rebecca a lot.

6. _____ Kevin isn't talking much.

7. _____ He's talked very little since his father's death.

8. _____ Everyone is worried about Kevin.

9. _____ Many people have called the Caseys.

10. _____ Anne feels bad for Kevin.

2. Change the full forms to contractions in the sentences below.

1. I have never visited California.   I've never visited California.

2. She has called three times today.   _____

3. We have talked to them before.   _____

4. It has rained all day.   _____

5. He has liked them for a long time.   _____

6. I have walked for ten miles.   _____

7. You have looked at this before.   _____

3. Complete the sentences with *have* or *has*.

1. She _has_ lived here for many years.

2. They _____ talked to us twice today.

3. You _____ wanted a house for two years.

4. We _____ visited them before.

5. It _____ snowed a lot this year.

6. She _____ listened to everything.

POWER Practice

4. What have you and your friends or family talked about? Write six sentences. Use the present perfect tense.

Examples: I have talked about my job with my friend. My brother has talked to me about his trip.

1. _____

2. _____

3. _____

4. _____

5. _____

6. _____

5. What has happened in your life this week? Write six sentences in the present perfect tense. Use the regular verbs in the box or use your own words. Use your own paper.

Examples: I have looked at a new car. My mother has visited me.

look	call	listen	walk	wash
visit	watch	clean	study	talk

ADVERBIALS WITH PRESENT PERFECT TENSE

FOR/SINCE WITH PRESENT PERFECT TENSE				
SUBJECT	**HAVE / HAS**	**PAST PARTICIPLE**		**[FOR + Amount of Time]**
I We You They	have	lived gone been	for	ten years. two months. a long time. one week.
			there	**[SINCE + Specific Time/Day/Date/Event]**
He She It	has		since	1990. last Monday. the election. January 10.

JUST WITH PRESENT PERFECT TENSE			
SUBJECT	**HAVE / HAS**	**JUST**	**PAST PARTICIPLE**
I, We, You, They	have	just	finished.
He, She, It	has		eaten.

IRREGULAR VERBS	
SIMPLE FORM	**PAST PARTICIPLE**
be	been
bring	brought
eat	eaten
feel	felt
give	given
go	gone
have	had
hear	heard
know	known
make	made
put	put
read	read
say	said
see	seen
speak	spoken
take	taken
think	thought
tell	told

NOTES

- We use some common adverbial expressions with the present perfect tense.
  – We use [**for** + amount of time]: *He has worked there for three years.*
  – We use [**since** + specific time/day/ date/event]: *He has worked there since 1995.*
  – We use **just** for recent past actions: *We have just moved to a new house.*

Kevin: *Mrs. Peterson **has just given** this to us. I'll put it in the fridge.*

Practice

6. Underline the adverbial expressions with *for* or *since*. Circle the adverbial *just*.

1. Rebecca's lived in Boston <u>for 27 years</u>.

2. Kevin's (just) talked to Mrs. Peterson.

3. Rebecca's looked at cards for two hours.

4. Brendan's talked to Anne for an hour.

5. Rebecca has just opened a letter.

6. Rebecca's been sad since last week.

7. Kevin has just put food in the fridge.

8. Brendan's read many cards since the funeral.

7. Complete the sentences with *for*, *since*, or *just*.

1. I've been in Boston <u>for</u> ten years.

2. We've _____ eaten dinner.

3. She's spoken French _____ 1996.

4. I've heard that _____ three days.

5. He has felt bad _____ Tuesday.

6. They've _____ seen us.

7. I have known them _____ June.

8. We've _____ told her the answer.

8. Put the words in the correct order. Write sentences in the present perfect tense.

1. have / weeks / they / for / known / three   They have known for three weeks.

2. just / she / finished / work / has / the   _____

3. we / since / been / 1990 / have / here   _____

4. for / had / ten / he / years / has / it   _____

5. rained / since / it / yesterday / has / twice   _____

6. they / seen / just / him / have   _____

9. Complete the sentences. Write the present perfect tense of the verbs in parentheses.

1. (go) She __has gone_____ to the store.

2. (have) I _____ a headache for three hours.

3. (be) It _____ cold since Tuesday.

4. (see) They _____ that movie.

5. (tell) You _____ me the same story for years.

6. (make) He _____ chairs since 1990.

POWER Practice

10. Write six sentences about your life. Write about actions or situations that began in the past and continue now. Use the present perfect tense + *for* or *since*.

Examples: *I've worked as a doctor for ten years. I've lived in Chicago since 1980.*

1. _____

2. _____

3. _____

4. _____

5. _____

6. _____

11. Write six sentences about your recent past. Use the present perfect tense + *just*. Use your own paper.

Examples: *I've just finished my homework. I've just visited New York.*

PRESENT PERFECT TENSE AND SIMPLE PAST TENSE

PRESENT PERFECT TENSE		
SUBJECT	*HAVE/HAS*	PAST PARTICIPLE
We	**have**	
		been	here since 1990.
She	**has**	

SIMPLE PAST TENSE		
SUBJECT	SIMPLE PAST TENSE FORM	
We	**were**	there in 1995.
She	**was**	there from 1990 to 1995.

IRREGULAR VERBS		
SIMPLE FORM	SIMPLE PAST TENSE FORM	PAST PARTICIPLE
be	was/were	been
bring	brought	brought
eat	ate	eaten
feel	felt	felt
give	gave	given
go	went	gone
have	had	had
know	knew	known
say	said	said
see	saw	seen
speak	spoke	spoken
take	took	taken
think	thought	thought
tell	told	told

NOTES

- We use the **present perfect tense** for actions and situations that began in the past and continue into the present. We *cannot* use the **simple past tense** for these actions and situations.
- We also use the **present perfect tense** for actions and situations that happened in the past. We don't say *when* they happened: *I've finished.*
- We use the **simple past tense** for actions and situations that began and ended in the past.

Rebecca **has been worried** about Kevin.

Rebecca **asked** Kevin about his future plans.

Practice

12. Underline the present perfect tense verbs. Circle the simple past tense verbs.

1. Kevin has finished high school.
2. Rebecca (talked) to Kevin about college yesterday.
3. Mr. Casey talked about an insurance policy before he died.
4. Kevin and Rebecca have looked in their father's room.
5. Rebecca has received many cards.
6. Kevin and Rebecca ate a pizza together.

13. Circle the correct verb tense in the sentences below.

1. I was / (have been) here since Monday.
2. She saw / has seen him yesterday.
3. We knew / have known Karen since 1995.
4. We ate / have eaten there last night.
5. He felt / has felt sick since lunch.
6. She spoke / has spoken to me last week.
7. You had / have had that car since 1997.
8. I heard / have heard the news last night.

14. Complete the sentences with the words in the box.

has lived	called	traveled	have worked
visited	has wanted	was	have seen

1. They _called_____ him after class.

2. She _____ in this town since 1990.

3. I _____ with them last year.

4. They _____ at the same company for five months.

5. We _____ Paris three years ago.

6. He _____ a new car for three months.

7. They _____ six movies since December.

8. It _____ really cold last week!

Practice

15. Tell a story about last weekend. Write six sentences. Use the simple past tense.

Examples: *I visited my friends. We cooked Chinese food for dinner.*

1. _____

2. _____

3. _____

4. _____

5. _____

6. _____

16. Write four sentences about things you have always liked. Write four sentences about things you have always disliked. Use the present perfect tense. Use your own paper.

Examples: *I have always liked bicycles.*

I have always disliked spinach.

A BOX OF MEMORIES

PRESENT PERFECT TENSE, NEGATIVE STATEMENTS

NEGATIVE STATEMENTS			
SUBJECT	*HAVE/HAS + NOT*	**PAST PARTICIPLE**	
I		**been**	there.
We	**have not**	**eaten**	dinner yet.
You	**haven't**	**started**	the project.
They		**visited**	Canada.
He	**has not**	**finished**	it yet.
She	**hasn't**		
It			

📋 NOTES

• We use [subject + auxiliary verb **have/has** + **not** + past participle of main verb] for negative statements in the present perfect tense.

• We use the negative contractions **haven't** or **hasn't** in conversation and in informal writing.

• We can use **yet** in negative statements about actions or situations that haven't happened but might happen in the future: *They haven't left yet.*

Rebecca and Kevin **haven't looked** in the safe deposit box yet.

Practice

1. Check (✔) the negative statements in the present perfect tense. Underline the full forms. Circle the present perfect verbs with contractions.

1. ✔ Rebecca <u>has not looked</u> at the papers.

2. ✔ Kevin (hasn't talked) to the bank officer.

3. _____ Rebecca didn't know about the box.

4. _____ They aren't rich.

5. _____ They haven't seen the ring before.

6. _____ Kevin doesn't want to leave Boston.

7. _____ They have not told Brendan yet.

8. _____ Rebecca hasn't made a decision.

2. Change the full forms to contractions.

1. We have not walked for three days. _We haven't walked for three days._

2. She has not called me since Tuesday. _____

3. They have not visited us for a year. _____

4. It has not rained since August. _____

5. You have not done your work. _____

6. I have not talked to them for a long time. _____

3. Circle the correct auxiliary verb in each sentence below.

1. I hasn't / (haven't) gone to Los Angeles yet.

2. She hasn't / haven't seen this book.

3. We hasn't / haven't eaten breakfast.

4. They hasn't / haven't called us.

5. It hasn't / haven't snowed this year.

6. You hasn't / haven't finished your work.

4. Change these sentences from affirmative to negative. Use contractions.

1. She's wanted a dog for a long time.   *She hasn't wanted a dog for a long time.*

2. We've made those before.   _____

3. He's gone there for years.   _____

4. I've been to her house since the party.   _____

5. They've talked about him for an hour.   _____

6. It's snowed for three days.   _____

7. You've done that before.   _____

POWER Practice

5. Think about things you have not done in the past. Write five sentences. Use negative statements in the present perfect tense.

Examples: I haven't visited Asia. I haven't eaten oysters.

1. _____

2. _____

3. _____

4. _____

5. _____

6. Think about your family members and your friends. Think about things they have wanted to do for a long time, but haven't done. Write six sentences about them. Use negative statements in the present perfect tense. Use your own paper.

Examples: My parents haven't had a vacation.   My sister hasn't been to college.

PRESENT PERFECT TENSE, *YES/NO* QUESTIONS AND SHORT ANSWERS

YES/NO QUESTIONS			
HAVE / HAS	**SUBJECT**	**PAST PARTICIPLE**	
Have	I we you they	**bought**	a new car?
		played	tennis?
		called	them?
		gone	home yet?
Has	he she it	**looked**	for it?

SHORT ANSWERS		
YES / NO	**SUBJECT**	**HAVE / HAS (+ NOT)**
Yes,	I, we, you, they	**have.**
	he, she, it	**has.**
No,	I, we, you, they	**have not. haven't.**
	he, she, it	**has not. hasn't.**

📝 NOTES

- We use [auxiliary verb **Have/Has** + subject + past participle of main verb] for **Yes/No** questions in the present perfect tense.
- We use [subject + **have/has**] for short answers with **Yes** in the present perfect tense.
- We use [subject + **have/has** + **not**] for short answers with **No** in the present perfect tense.
- We can use **yet** in **Yes/No** questions to ask about actions or situations we expect to happen: *Have you done your homework yet?*

Rebecca: ***Have** you **looked** at this?*

Kevin: *No, I **haven't**.*

Practice

7. Check (✔) the *Yes/No* questions in the present perfect tense.

✔ **1.** Has Rebecca been to the bank?

____ **2.** Has Rebecca told Uncle Brendan yet?

____ **3.** Kevin hasn't seen his friends.

____ **4.** Has Kevin seen this ring?

____ **5.** Have Kevin and Rebecca talked about college?

____ **6.** Kevin and Rebecca haven't left Boston.

8. Circle the correct verb forms in the questions below.

1. (Have) / Has Rebecca and Kevin looked for an insurance policy?

2. Have / Has Rebecca called the insurance company?

3. Have / Has Rebecca and Kevin decided about their future?

4. Have / Has Kevin listened to Rebecca?

5. Have / Has Rebecca spoken to Brendan and Anne?

9. Match the questions and short answers.

_c_ **1.** Have you finished your work?

_____ **2.** Has he read this yet?

_____ **3.** Have they visited you since last year?

_____ **4.** Has it rained today?

_____ **5.** Has she eaten here before?

_____ **6.** Have we been to his house yet?

a. Yes, she has.

b. No, we haven't.

✔**c.** Yes, I have.

d. No, he hasn't.

e. Yes, they have.

f. No, it hasn't.

10. Put the words in order. Write *Yes/No* questions.

1. yet / she / car / seen / our / has / new

Has she seen our new car yet?

2. have / before / called / us / they

_____

3. since / he / has / you / visited / 1990

_____

4. homework / you / done / your / have / yet

_____

5. June / been / has / since / it / hot

_____

POWER Practice

11. Write six *Yes/No* questions for your friend. Has he/she done anything interesting? Use the present perfect tense.

Examples: *Have you talked to a famous person? Have you visited Paris?*

1. _____

2. _____

3. _____

4. _____

5. _____

6. _____

12. PRETEND: You are going to talk to a famous person. Write six *Yes/No* questions about his/her life. Use the present perfect tense. Use your own paper.

Examples: *Have you traveled to interesting places? Have you earned a lot of money?*

PRESENT PERFECT TENSE, *WH-* QUESTIONS

WH-QUESTION WORD	HAVE/HAS	SUBJECT	PAST PARTICIPLE
Who Whom	has	she	called?
What	have	you	eaten?
When	have	they	helped?
Where	has	it	gone?
How long	has	he	known?

NOTES

- We use [**Wh-** question word + auxiliary verb **have/has** + subject + past participle of main verb] for information questions in the present perfect tense.
- We use **Who** in conversation and in informal writing. We use **Whom** in formal writing and in formal speaking.
- We can use **How long** in **Wh-** questions in the present perfect tense. **How long** asks how much time has passed from the beginning of an action to the present.

Kevin: ***Who have*** you ***talked*** to about this?

Rebecca: *I haven't talked to anyone yet.*

Practice

13. Check (✔) the *Wh-* questions in the present perfect tense.

✔ **1.** What have Rebecca and Kevin taken to the bank?

____ **2.** When did Rebecca talk to the bank officer?

____ **3.** What has Rebecca seen at the bank?

____ **4.** What did the bank officer ask Rebecca for?

____ **5.** Where have Rebecca and Kevin looked at the safe deposit box?

____ **6.** What has Rebecca found in the box?

14. Match the questions and answers.

_b_ **1.** How long have you known him?

____ **2.** What have they made for dinner?

____ **3.** Who has she helped?

____ **4.** How long has she lived here?

____ **5.** Where have they traveled?

____ **6.** What have you planted?

a. All over South America.

✔**b.** I've known him for three years.

c. Since 1997.

d. Roses.

e. Her brothers.

f. Spaghetti.

15. Complete the questions with *Who*, *What*, *When*, *Where*, or *How long*.

1. __Where__ have you worked?   I've worked in London and Tokyo.

2. _____ has he seen?   He's seen his mother and father.

3. _____ have they made for dinner?   They've made chicken and rice.

4. _____ has she lived in New York?   She's lived in New York for ten years.

5. _____ has your cousin gone?   He's gone back home.

6. _____ have you been?   I've been to Italy and Greece.

7. _____ have you invited to the party?   We've invited all of our friends.

8. _____ has she known you?   She's known me since 1990.

9. _____ have they helped you?   They've helped me many times.

10. _____ has he studied?   He's studied biology and economics.

POWER Practice

16. Answer these questions. Use the present perfect tense.

Example: *How long have you studied English?   I've studied English for two years.*

1. How long have you studied English?   _____

2. Where have you studied English?   _____

3. What have you learned this year?   _____

4. Who have you seen today?   _____

17. What places has your friend visited? Write five questions for your friend. Use *Who*, *What*, *When*, *Where*, and *How long*.

Examples: *Where have you visited in the United States?*

Who have you traveled with?

1. _____

2. _____

3. _____

4. _____

5. _____

THE MISSING CAR

PRESENT PERFECT CONTINUOUS TENSE, AFFIRMATIVE STATEMENTS

FULL FORMS			
SUBJECT	**HAVE / HAS**	**BEEN**	**MAIN VERB + -ING**
I We You They	have		
		been	working.
He She It	has		

CONTRACTIONS		
[SUBJECT + HAVE / HAS]	**BEEN**	**MAIN VERB + -ING**
I've We've You've They've		
	been	working.
He's She's It's		

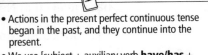

NOTES

- Actions in the present perfect continuous tense began in the past, and they continue into the present.
- We use [subject + auxiliary verb **have/has** + **been** + simple form of main verb + **-ing**] for affirmative statements in the present perfect continuous tense.
- We use contractions in conversation and in informal writing.

They've been eating lunch.
Brendan **has been talking** about the ring.

Practice

1. Check (✔) the sentences in the present perfect continuous tense.

1. ✔ They have been having lunch together.

2. _____ They were eating oysters.

3. _____ They have given Brendan a ring.

4. _____ They've been discussing the future.

5. _____ They have to make some plans.

6. _____ Kevin has been listening to them.

7. _____ He's been thinking a lot.

8. _____ He's going to walk home.

2. Put the words in order. Write sentences in the present perfect continuous tense.

1. have / they / Texas / living / in / been   They have been living in Texas.

2. been / she / studying / has _____

3. our / we / doing / homework / been / have _____

4. has / washing / dishes / he / the / been _____

5. he / writing / book / a / been / has _____

6. talking / we / been / have / more _____

7. have / you / trying / hard / been _____

3. Write six sentences with words from the box. Use full verb forms. Then rewrite your sentences with *He*, *She*, or *They* and use contractions.

Alicia		collecting money for their class trip
My grandparents		doing her homework
My parents	have been	sending me postcards from their trip
The President	has been	speaking on TV
Those kids		visiting my grandparents
Your brother		washing his car

1. _Alicia has been doing her homework. She's been doing her homework._

2. _____

3. _____

4. _____

5. _____

6. _____

4. Complete the sentences. Use the present perfect continuous tense. Use contractions.

1. The girls are singing. _They've been singing_ for an hour.

2. The men are working hard. _____ hard all day.

3. We're talking about moving. _____ about it for weeks.

4. Joe is watching T.V. _____ T.V. since 7:00.

5. She's studying. _____ for hours.

6. I'm practicing the guitar. _____ a lot lately.

POWER Practice

5. Write about six friends. What has each friend been doing? Use the present perfect continuous tense. Use your own paper.

Example: Michelle has been writing letters to her boyfriend.

6. Write six sentences about you and your family. What have you been doing? Use the present perfect continuous tense. Use your own paper.

Examples: I've been watching Episode 32.   My sisters have been planning a trip.

PRESENT PERFECT CONTINUOUS TENSE, NEGATIVE STATEMENTS

FULL FORMS				
SUBJECT	**HAVE / HAS**	**NOT**	**BEEN**	**MAIN VERB + -ING**
I We You They	have	not	been	working.
He She It	has			

CONTRACTIONS			
SUBJECT	**[HAVE / HAS + NOT]**	**BEEN**	**MAIN VERB + -ING**
I We You They	haven't	been	working.
He She It	hasn't		

NOTES

- We use [subject + auxiliary verb **have/has** + **not** + **been** + simple form of main verb + **-ing**] for negative statements in the present perfect continuous tense.
- We use contractions in conversation and in informal writing.

Kevin and Rebecca **have not been getting along** well.

Kevin **hasn't been talking** about his feelings.

Practice

7. Check (✔) the negative sentences in the present perfect continuous tense.

1. ✔ They have not been arguing at lunch.

2. _____ Anne hasn't been eating oysters.

3. _____ Brendan has seen the ring.

4. _____ He hasn't been driving his own car.

5. _____ They have been staying in a hotel.

6. _____ Kevin has not been cleaning his room.

7. _____ They haven't been seeing their friends.

8. _____ Kevin hasn't decided to go to college.

8. Complete the sentences. Use the full forms *have not been* or *has not been* in 1-4. Use the contractions *haven't been* or *hasn't been* in 5-8.

1. We _have not been_____ studying chemistry.

2. He _____ sleeping well.

3. My mother _____ making my lunch.

4. My father _____ working on weekends.

5. Bob and Tina _haven't been_____ exercising.

6. Edith _____ practicing the piano.

7. You and I _____ getting together very often.

8. I _____ feeling well.

9. Write negative statements. Use the present perfect continuous tense. Use full forms in 1-5. Use contractions in 6-10.

1. We / live / in New York City _We have not been living in New York City._

2. They / eat / in restaurants _____

3. She / take / photographs _____

4. He / study / for his test _____

5. I / wait / for you _____

6. Roberta / drive / her car _Roberta hasn't been driving her car._

7. Sharon and Michael / eat / meat _____

8. You and I / go / to the movies _____

9. My car / run / well _____

10. You / read / much _____

POWER Practice

10. Think about **good** things you haven't been doing. Write six negative sentences in the present perfect continuous tense. Use the words in the box, or use your own words. Use your own paper.

do my homework	sleep well	save money	call my mother
enjoy my weekends	eat well	see my friends	practice English

Example: *I haven't been exercising.*

11. Think about **bad** things you haven't been doing. Write six negative sentences in the present perfect continuous tense. Use the words in the box, or use your own words. Use your own paper.

stay up late	spend too much money	forget my homework	avoid my friends
eat junk food	watch too much TV	bite my fingernails	ignore my family

Example: *I haven't been wasting my time.*

COMPARATIVE AND SUPERLATIVE ADJECTIVES

SIMPLE FORMS	COMPARATIVE FORMS			SUPERLATIVE FORMS		NOTES
ADJECTIVES WITH ONE SYLLABLE	[ADJECTIVE + -ER] + *THAN*			*THE* + [ADJECTIVE + *-EST*]		• We use the comparative form of an adjective for comparisons of two people, ideas, or things.
big small young	**bigger** **smaller** **younger**		**than**	**the**	**biggest** **smallest** **youngest**	• We use [comparative adjective + **than**]: *July is hotter than May.*
SOME ADJECTIVES WITH TWO SYLLABLES	[ADJECTIVE + -ER] + *THAN*			*THE* + [ADJECTIVE + *-EST*]		• We use the superlative form of an adjective for comparisons of more than two people, ideas, or things.
easy funny happy narrow pretty quiet	**easier** **funnier** **happier** **narrower** **prettier** **quieter**		**than**	**the**	**easiest** **funniest** **happiest** **narrowest** **prettiest** **quietest**	• We use [**the** + superlative adjective]: *February is the shortest month of the year.*
ADJECTIVES WITH TWO OR MORE SYLLABLES	*MORE* + ADJECTIVE + *THAN*			*THE MOST* + ADJECTIVE		• Some irregular comparative and superlative adjectives are:
beautiful crowded difficult famous interesting	**more**	**beautiful** **crowded** **difficult** **famous** **interesting**	**than**	**the most**	**beautiful** **crowded** **difficult** **famous** **interesting**	**bad, worse, worst** **good, better, best**

The Union Oyster House is **older than** any other restaurant in Boston.

It is **the oldest** restaurant in Boston.

Practice

12. Underline the comparative adjectives. Circle the superlative adjectives.

1. Kevin and Rebecca feel <u>richer than</u> before.

2. Anne is (the quietest) person at the table.

3. Brendan was more successful than Patrick.

4. Rebecca is older than her brother.

5. Kevin is taller than Rebecca.

6. Rebecca is the best musician in her family.

13. Complete the sentences with comparative adjectives + *than*.

1. Your car is new. It is _newer than_____ my car.

2. The second test was difficult. It was _____ the first test.

3. Her story is good. It's _____ my story.

4. Today's class was interesting. It was _____ Tuesday's class.

5. The Greens seem very happy. They seem _____ the Smiths.

14. Complete the sentences with superlative adjectives.

1. All of our cars are fast. My cousin's car is _the fastest_ of all.

2. All our teachers are good. My teacher is _____ teacher of all.

3. Todd, Scott, and my brother are funny. My brother is _____ of the three.

4. All of the apartments are quiet. This one is _____ apartment of them all.

5. That was a difficult chapter. It was _____ chapter in the book.

15. Complete the sentences. Use the comparative or superlative form of the adjective.

	CHINA	INDIA	THE UNITED STATES
Population	1,243,700,000	960,200,000	271,600,000
Area (square miles)	9,597,000	1,269,000	3,619,000
Longest river (length in miles)	Yangtze: 3,960	Indus: 1,925	Mississippi: 3,740
Highest mountain (height in feet)	Everest: 29,029	Kanchenjunga: 28,208	McKinley: 20,321

1. (large) The population of India is _larger than_ the population of the U.S.

2. (large) China has _the largest_ population of the three countries.

3. (big) The U.S. is _____ India.

4. (big) China is _____ of the three countries.

5. (long) The Mississippi River is _____ the Indus.

6. (long) The Yangtze is _____ of the three rivers.

7. (high) Mt. Kanchenjunga is _____ Mt. McKinley.

8. (high) Mt. Everest is _____ of the three mountains.

POWER Practice

16. Write five comparative and five superlative sentences about people you know.
Use the adjectives *beautiful, funny, generous, intelligent,* and *quiet*. Use your own paper.

Examples: My mother is more beautiful than my aunt. My grandmother is the most beautiful of all.

17. Think of three cities. Write five comparative and five superlative sentences about them. Use the adjectives *crowded, expensive, friendly, interesting,* and *safe*. Use your own paper.

Examples: Washington is more crowded than Austin. New York is the most crowded of the three cities.

A **B**REAKDOWN

PRESENT PERFECT CONTINUOUS TENSE, *YES/NO* QUESTIONS AND SHORT ANSWERS

YES/NO QUESTIONS

HAVE / HAS	SUBJECT	BEEN	MAIN VERB + -ING	
Have	I we you they	**been**	**working**	well?
Has	he she it			

SHORT ANSWERS

YES/NO	SUBJECT	HAVE / HAS (+ NOT)
Yes,	I, we, you, they	**have**.
	he, she, it	**has**.
No,	I, we, you, they	**have not**. **haven't**.
	he, she, it	**has not**. **hasn't**.

📝 NOTES

- Actions in the present perfect continuous tense began in the past, and they continue into the present.
- We use [auxiliary verb **Have/Has** + subject + **been** + simple form of main verb + **-ing**] for **Yes/No** questions in the present perfect continuous tense.
- Short answers in the present perfect continuous tense are like short answers in the present perfect tense.

Have they *been talking* about their relationship?
Yes, they *have*.
Has Kevin *been asking* Laura about college?
No, he *hasn't*.

Practice

1. Check (✔) the *Yes/No* questions in the present perfect continuous tense.

1. __✔__ Have Kevin and Laura been talking?

2. _____ Has he been asking her about college?

3. _____ Have they been watching the airplanes?

4. _____ Has Kevin been seeing other girls?

5. _____ Has Rebecca called the police?

6. _____ Did Kevin take Brendan's car?

7. _____ Has Laura been writing to him?

8. _____ Have they been talking about their relationship?

2. Circle the correct short answers to these *Yes/No* questions about the story.

1. Has Laura been seeing other guys?   (Yes, she has.)/ Yes, she was.

2. Has she been writing to Kevin?   No, she isn't. / No, she hasn't.

3. Has Rebecca been calling Kevin's friends?   Yes, she does. / Yes, she has.

4. Have they been listening for the car?   Yes, they are. / Yes, they have.

5. Have they been looking for Kevin?   No, they haven't. / No, they aren't.

3. Put the words in order. Add *Has* or *Have*, and write *Yes/No* questions in the present perfect continuous tense.

1. been / she / studying ____ Has she been studying? ____

2. shopping / been / they ____

3. it / been / raining ____

4. well / car / running / your / been ____

5. you / my / been / using / radio ____

6. been / college / you / thinking / about ____

4. Change the statements to *Yes/No* questions. Then write short answers.

1. She hasn't been buying clothes. ___ Has she been buying clothes? No, she hasn't. ___

2. We've been saving money. ____

3. My cold hasn't been getting better. ____

4. I haven't been getting my mail. ____

5. Rob has been learning Spanish. ____

6. We've been planning a trip to Mexico. ____

POWER Practice

5. Answer the questions about your life in the last two years.

Example: *Have you been working? Yes, I have. (or) No, I haven't.*

1. Have you been studying? ____

2. Have you been reading a lot? ____

3. Have you been traveling? ____

4. Have you been playing a sport? ____

5. Have you been living alone? ____

6. Have you been making new friends? ____

6. PRETEND: Your friend has moved away. Find out about your friend's new life. Write six *Yes/No* questions in the present perfect continuous tense. Use your own paper.

Example: *Have you been working hard?*

PRESENT PERFECT CONTINUOUS TENSE, *WH-* QUESTIONS

WH- QUESTION WORD OR PHRASE	HAVE / HAS	SUBJECT	BEEN	MAIN VERB + -ING
Who Whom	has	she		calling?
What	has	he		doing?
Where	have	they	been	staying?
How long	have	they		visiting?

NOTES

- Actions in the present perfect continuous tense began in the past, and they continue into the present.
- We use [**Wh-** question word or phrase + auxiliary verb **have/has** + subject + **been** + simple form of main verb + **-ing**] for information questions in the present perfect continuous tense.
- We use **Who** in conversation and in informal writing. We use **Whom** in formal writing and in formal speaking.

Who has Rebecca **been talking** to?
Sandy.
How long have they **been worrying** about Kevin?
For several hours.

Practice

7. Check the *Wh-* questions in the present perfect continuous tense.

1. ✔ Who has Rebecca been talking to?
2. ____ What has she been saying?
3. ____ Where has Kevin been?
4. ____ What has he been doing?

5. ____ What is Jack doing?
6. ____ How long have they been there?
7. ____ Where have they been staying?
8. ____ Where are they going?

8. Match the *Wh-* questions and answers.

1. _g_ Where have you been living?
2. ____ How long have you been living there?
3. ____ What have you been doing?
4. ____ Who has he been seeing?
5. ____ How long have I been reading?
6. ____ Where have you been studying?
7. ____ Who has been teaching Spanish?
8. ____ What has he been studying?

a. At City College.
b. His new girlfriend.
c. Chemistry.
d. For two months.
e. I've been taking a vacation.
f. Professor Jackson.
✔ g. On Green Street.
h. For an hour.

9. Write eight **Wh-** questions with words and phrases from the box. Use the present perfect continuous tense.

Who		you		doing	speaking
What		the President		going	speaking to
Where	have	that woman	been	listening	waiting for
How long	has	your classmates		listening to	working
				living	working with
				living here	

1. <u>Who have you been speaking to?</u>

2. _____

3. _____

4. _____

5. _____

6. _____

7. _____

8. _____

10. Put the words in order. Add **have** or **has** + **been**. Write **Wh-** questions in the present perfect continuous tense.

1. you / where / living

   <u>Where have you been living?</u>

2. burning / the fire / how long

   _____

3. what / doing / they

   _____

4. seeing / you / who

   _____

5. they / skiing / how long

   _____

6. where / eating / you / breakfast

   _____

Practice

11. PRETEND: It's the weekend and you have been out all day. What has your family been doing? Write 10 questions for members of your family. Use **Wh-** questions and the present perfect continuous tense. Use your own paper.

	Person:	Question:
Examples:	Father:	*What games have you been watching on TV?*
	Sister:	*Who have you been talking to on the phone?*

REVIEW: DIRECT OBJECT INFINITIVES: AFFIRMATIVE AND NEGATIVE STATEMENTS; *YES/NO* QUESTIONS

	SUBJECT	AUX.	MAIN VERB	DIRECT OBJECT INFINITIVE
AFFIRMATIVE STATEMENTS	She		likes	**to sing.**
	They	should	offer	**to help.**
NEGATIVE STATEMENTS	He	doesn't	want	**to play.**
	You	didn't	need	**to explain.**

	AUX.	SUBJECT	MAIN VERB	DIRECT OBJECT INFINITIVE
YES/NO QUESTIONS	Do	they	need	**to talk?**
	Will	he	want	**to go?**
	Did	you	like	**to study?**
	Has	she	refused	**to apologize?**

📝 NOTES

- An infinitive is [**to** + simple form of verb].
- An infinitive can be the direct object of the main verb in a sentence. It follows the verb: *They like to ski.*
- A direct object infinitive can have words after the verb: *They like to ski at night.*
- Some common verbs with direct object infinitives are **begin, continue, decide, expect, hate, hope, learn, like, love, need, offer, plan, promise, refuse, start,** and **want.**
- AUX. = auxiliary verb.

Rebecca wanted **to sing**. Kevin didn't refuse **to listen**. They are learning **to talk** to each other again.

Practice

12. Underline the direct object infinitives.

1. Laura has begun <u>to see</u> other guys.

2. Kevin didn't expect to be out of her life.

3. Anne and Brendan are planning to go home soon.

4. They need to return to the farm.

5. They have offered to take Rebecca and Kevin.

6. Rebecca needs to ask Kevin about it.

13. Complete the statements with the main verb and a direct object infinitive.

1. (want / buy) He <u>wanted to buy</u> _____ some new clothes.

2. (need / study) We _____ for our test.

3. (expect / pass) I _____ the test easily.

4. (plan / meet) She _____ me at six o'clock.

5. (refuse / watch) He _____ the movie.

14. Look at the answers below. Write *Yes/No* questions for these answers.

1. (forget / lock) <u>Did you forget to lock</u> _____ the car?   No, we didn't.

2. (like / clean) _____ his room?   No, he doesn't.

3. (love / laugh) _____ ?   Yes, they do.

4. (hate / buy) _____ new clothes?   No, she doesn't.

5. (promise / come) _____ with us?   Yes, I will.

6. (hope / find) _____ a better life?   Yes, they did.

POWER Practice

15. Write sentences about your likes and dislikes ten years ago. Write sentences about your likes and dislikes now. Use direct object infinitives. Use the verbs in the box.

hate	like	love

Examples: *Ten years ago, I hated to eat fish.   Now I love to eat fish.*
              I didn't like to swim.   I don't like to dance.

TEN YEARS AGO:

1. _____

2. _____

3. _____

4. _____

NOW:

5. _____

6. _____

7. _____

8. _____

16. Write four affirmative sentences and four negative sentences about your future. Use direct object infinitives. Use the verbs in the box. Use your own paper.

want	hope	plan	expect

Examples: *I want to live in another country.   I don't want to be poor.*

A CALL FOR HELP

DIRECT OBJECT GERUNDS: AFFIRMATIVE AND NEGATIVE STATEMENTS

	SUBJECT	MAIN VERB	DIRECT OBJECT GERUND	
AFFIRMATIVE STATEMENTS	They	begin	**studying**	after dinner.
	She	continued	**talking**	in Thai.

	SUBJECT	AUX. + NOT	MAIN VERB	DIRECT OBJECT GERUND
NEGATIVE STATEMENTS	We	don't	like	**practicing.**
	He	hasn't	enjoyed	**walking.**

📝 **NOTES**

• A gerund is [verb + **-ing**].
• We use a gerund in place of a noun to name a situation or an action.
• A direct object gerund follows the main verb in the sentence: *We continued practicing.*
• A direct object gerund can have words after it: *We continued practicing English.*
• Some common verbs with direct object gerunds are **begin**, **continue**, **dislike**, **enjoy**, **finish**, **hate**, **like**, **love**, **practice**, and **start**.

The Caseys enjoy **having** breakfast together.

Practice

1. Underline the main verb and circle the direct object gerund in each sentence.

1. Uncle Brendan <u>enjoys</u> (working) on the farm.

2. Sandy won't continue living with Jack.

3. Kevin will try living on his uncle's farm.

4. Rebecca practices playing the guitar every day.

5. Rebecca hasn't stopped thinking about music school.

2. Match the two parts of the sentences. Write the letters.

1. _d_ Rebecca doesn't practice

2. ____ Sandy hates

3. ____ Anne enjoys

4. ____ Uncle Brendan won't stop

5. ____ Rebecca began

a. helping Rebecca and Kevin.

b. visiting Boston with Brendan.

c. living with Jack now.

✔ **d.** playing the piano.

e. studying at the college in September.

3. Complete the sentences. Use the verbs in parentheses as a direct object gerunds.

1. (talk) Please stop _talking_____.

2. (study) They won't continue _____ Spanish next year.

3. (take) I begin _____ my exams tomorrow.

4. (play) She never practices _____ the piano.

5. (speak) They haven't started _____ English at home.

6. (listen) She likes _____ to classical music.

7. (eat) We finished _____ early yesterday.

8. (read) You started _____ that book last week.

9. (write) Yoshi likes _____ poetry.

10. (plan) She doesn't like _____ a party.

4. Write sentences with direct object gerunds.

1. I / enjoy / swim   _I enjoy swimming._____

2. Marta / dislike / go / alone   _____

3. He / will / continue / practice / later   _____

4. They / do not / like / do / homework   _____

5. She / does not / begin / teach / tomorrow   _____

6. The students / began / arrive / yesterday   _____

POWER Practice

5. What do you enjoy doing? Make two lists. Write ten sentences with direct object gerunds. Use your own paper.

Examples: I enjoy swimming. I dislike washing dishes.

6. What should you change about your life? Write six promises about your future. Use the verbs in the box with direct object gerunds. Use your own paper.

begin	continue	practice	start

Examples: I will not start smoking. I will continue studying hard. I will begin exercising.

DIRECT OBJECT GERUNDS: *YES/NO* QUESTIONS AND SHORT ANSWERS

YES/NO QUESTIONS			
AUX.	SUBJECT	MAIN VERB	DIRECT OBJECT GERUND
Do	you	like	**skiing**?
Has	he	started	**practicing**?
Did	you	enjoy	**driving**?
Can	they	continue	**working**?
Will	she	practice	**singing**?
Should	we	begin	**reading**?

SHORT ANSWERS		
YES/NO	SUBJECT	AUX.
Yes,	I	do.
Yes,	he	has.
No,	I	didn't.
No,	they	can't.
Yes,	she	will.
No,	we	shouldn't.

NOTES
- We use [auxiliary verb + subject + main verb + gerund] in **Yes/No** questions with direct object gerunds.
- We use [subject + auxiliary verb] after **Yes/No** in short answers.
- A direct object gerund can have words after it: *Will she practice singing again?*

Rebecca: *Do you want to continue **living** with Jack?*

Sandy: *No, I don't.*

7. Underline the gerunds. Circle the correct answers.

1. Does Rebecca enjoy <u>studying</u> music? **a.** (Yes, she does.) **b.** Yes, she is.

2. Did Sandy like living with Jack? **a.** No, she wasn't. **b.** No, she didn't.

3. Should Sandy continue living with Jack? **a.** No, she isn't. **b.** No, she shouldn't.

4. Do Anne and Brendan like living on a farm? **a.** Yes, they do. **b.** Yes, they are.

5. Should Kevin start thinking about college? **a.** Yes, he will. **b.** Yes, he should.

6. Does Rebecca practice playing the guitar? **a.** Yes, she does. **b.** Yes, she is.

8. Change the sentences to *Yes/No* questions.

1. They enjoy walking in the woods. <u>Do they enjoy walking in the woods?</u>

2. Yoko started studying last week. _____

3. Pablo can begin working tomorrow. _____

4. Toshi and I can continue practicing later. _____

5. Her teacher likes leaving early. _____

6. We should stop talking in class. _____

9. Write **Yes/No** questions with direct object gerunds. Choose the main verbs and direct object gerunds from the boxes below. Write short answers to your questions.

begin	like
continue	love
dislike	practice
enjoy	start
finish	suggest

cooking	skiing
dancing	speaking
fishing	swimming
listening	teaching
reading	writing

1. Do you _like swimming? Yes, I do._____

2. Should she _____

3. Can they _____

4. Does he _____

5. Did they _____

6. Will you _____

7. Has she _____

8. Should they _____

9. Have you _____

10. Did she _____

POWER Practice

10. Write short answers to the questions.

Example: Can you start speaking English at work?   Yes, I can (or) No, I can't.

1. Do you enjoy studying English? _____

2. Should teachers stop giving homework? _____

3. Do you practice speaking English outside of class? _____

4. Will you continue studying English next year? _____

5. Can you try speaking English at home? _____

11. Write a survey for your friends. Choose a topic below. Then write six **Yes/No** questions. Use the verbs in the box and direct object gerunds. Use your own paper.

TOPICS: HOBBIES   GOOD HABITS   BAD HABITS

begin	start	enjoy	like	dislike	practice

Examples: Do you like watching television? Will you start exercising soon?

SUBJECT GERUNDS

SUBJECT GERUND	MAIN VERB	
Skiing	is	fun.
Taking a vacation	costs	money.
Giving speeches	seems	hard.

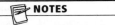 **NOTES**

- A subject gerund comes before the main verb in a sentence. It takes the subject position in a sentence.
- A gerund is always singular. A gerund takes the third person form of the main verb: *Studying takes time.*
- We can replace a gerund with **it:** *Learning a language is difficult, but it can be fun.*
- A subject gerund can have words after it: *Skiing at night is dangerous.*

Sandy didn't want to tell Jack her decision.
Telling him was difficult.

12. **Underline the subject gerunds. Circle the direct object gerunds.**

1. Living with Jack was dangerous for Sandy.

2. Jack should stop (drinking.)

3. Hitting Sandy was wrong.

4. Sandy finished packing quickly.

5. Leaving Jack wasn't easy for Sandy.

6. Rebecca liked helping her friend.

7. Kevin hates fighting.

8. Staying on the farm might be good for Kevin and Rebecca.

13. **Match the two parts of the sentences. Write the letters.**

1. _e_ Going to school

2. _____ Lifting weights

3. _____ Learning a new language

4. _____ Wearing new shoes

5. _____ Eating lots of desserts

6. _____ Calling my mother

a. can make your feet hurt.

b. makes me homesick.

c. is fattening.

d. can build your muscles.

✔e. costs a lot of money.

f. can be hard work.

14. Put the words in order. Write sentences with subject gerunds.

1. golf / is / playing / relaxing   Playing golf is relaxing.

2. good / you / exercising / for / is   _____

3. food / unusual / eating / is / for / him / spicy   _____

4. another / in / country / be / living / difficult / can   _____

5. expensive / long-distance / making / calls / is   _____

6. back / carrying / hurt / furniture / your / can   _____

15. Complete the conversation with subject or object gerunds. Use the verbs in the box.

complain	look	walk	read	shop	watch

Sally: *I'm bored. I'm going to watch television.*

Mother: __Watching_____ *television is bad for you, Sally. Why don't you go for a walk?*

Sally: *I don't like _____.*

Mother: *Well, I'm going to the library. You can go with me and get a book to read.*

Sally: *_____ is boring. I prefer to shop.*

Mother: *_____ is a waste of time. And you don't have any money.*

Sally: *I never have any money. I should start _____ for a job.*

Mother: *That's a good idea. Then maybe you will stop _____.*

POWER Practice

16. Write six sentences about your friends' favorite activities. Use subject gerunds. Use your own paper.

Example: *Swimming is Maria's favorite activity.   Reading is Toshi's favorite activity.*

17. What's your opinion about the activities below? Write six sentences about them. Use your own paper.

doing housework	doing homework	writing letters	working
studying	buying a car	smoking	cooking

Examples: *Doing homework is helpful.   Smoking is bad.*

ADVERBIAL PHRASES AND CLAUSES OF REASON: AFFIRMATIVE AND NEGATIVE STATEMENTS

MAIN CLAUSE		ADVERBIAL PHRASE OF REASON	
AFFIRMATIVE STATEMENTS	We stayed home	**because of** **due to**	**the weather**.
NEGATIVE STATEMENTS	We didn't go out		
MAIN CLAUSE		ADVERBIAL CLAUSE OF REASON	
AFFIRMATIVE STATEMENTS	They cancelled the baseball game	**since** **because**	**it was raining**.
NEGATIVE STATEMENTS	They didn't play baseball		

📝 NOTES

- A phrase is a group of words without [subject + verb].
- A clause is a group of words with [subject + verb].
- A sentence with an adverbial phrase or clause can tell the reason for an action or a situation in the main clause. It can answer the question **Why** about the main clause.
- An adverbial phrase or clause can come *before* or *after* the main clause of the sentence.
- We use a comma after an adverbial phrase or clause at the beginning of a sentence: *Because of the weather, we stayed home.*

The police arrested Jack **because he hit Sandy**.
Sandy is leaving **because of Jack's violence**.

Practice

1. Underline the adverbial phrases. Circle the adverbial clauses.

1. Sandy called the police because of Jack's threats.   **4.** Sandy went to a shelter because of Jack.

2. Jack was angry because Sandy was leaving him.   **5.** She needed the shelter due to her situation.

3. The police arrested Jack because he was violent.   **6.** She went alone since it was safer that way.

2. Match each main clause with the correct adverbial phrase or clause.

1. __c__ They're at the car dealer's because   **a.** an ad in the newspaper.

2. _____ They need a car because   **b.** they can't afford a new one.

3. _____ They chose this dealer due to   ✔**c.** they need to buy a car.

4. _____ They want a used car since   **d.** the high prices at the dealer's.

5. _____ They're upset because of   **e.** their old car broke down.

3. Rewrite each sentence with the adverbial phrase or clause at the beginning. Use commas.

   1. She went home because she felt sick. _Because she felt sick, she went home._

   2. The traffic was bad due to the snow. _____

   3. I drove slowly because of the road conditions. _____

   4. We had to hurry since they were waiting. _____

4. Write statements with words and phrases from the box.

She chose it	They wanted it	because	due to	its TV ads.	everyone liked it.
We went there	I like it	because of	since	it was beautiful.	the low price.

   1. _She chose it because it was beautiful._

   2. _____

   3. _____

   4. _____

   5. _____

   6. _____

POWER Practice

5. Complete the sentences about your likes and dislikes. Use words from the box or your own words. Add your reasons.

go to movies	listen to the radio	dance	go shopping	go to the beach

Example: *I like to listen to the radio because it relaxes me.*

   1. I like _____ because _____

   2. I don't like _____ because of _____

   3. I like _____ since _____

   4. I don't like _____ due to _____

6. Think of things you have done and not done in your life. Think about the reasons for your actions. Write four affirmative statements and four negative statements. Use adverbial phrases and clauses of reason. Use your own paper.

Examples: *I yelled at my little brother because he broke my CD player.*
I didn't pass chemistry because of my bad study habits.

ADVERBIAL PHRASES AND CLAUSES OF REASON: *YES/NO* QUESTIONS AND SHORT ANSWERS; *WH-* QUESTIONS WITH *WHY*

YES/NO QUESTIONS	ADVERBIAL PHRASE OF REASON	
Was she absent	**due to** **because of**	**the flu**?
Has she missed classes	**ADVERBIAL CLAUSE OF REASON**	
Did she see a doctor	**since** **because**	**she was sick**?

SHORT ANSWERS
Yes, she was.
Yes, she has.
No, she didn't.

📝 **NOTES**

- We can use adverbial phrases and clauses of reason in **Yes/No** questions to ask about the reason for an action or a situation.
- We also use the **Wh-** question word **Why** to ask about reasons.
- We use adverbial phrases and clauses to answer **Wh-** questions with **Why** in conversation. But they are not complete sentences, and we do not use them in formal writing.

WH- QUESTIONS WITH *WHY*			
WHY	AUX.	SUBJECT	MAIN VERB
Why	are	you	smiling?
	did	he	laugh?

ADVERBIAL PHRASE/CLAUSE
Because of your funny hat.
Because you're wearing a funny hat.

Why did Ramón write to Rebecca?
Because Alex asked him to.

Did Alex draw the picture **because he missed Rebecca**?
Yes, he did.

Practice

7. Check the questions with adverbial phrases or clauses of reason.

1. __✔__ Are Rebecca and Kevin packing because they're leaving the apartment?

2. _____ Is Rebecca going to the farm because of her concern for Kevin?

3. _____ Was Rebecca surprised to get Ramón's letter?

4. _____ Did Ramón write to her because of Alex?

5. _____ Will Rebecca see Sandy before she leaves?

8. Change the statements to *Yes/No* questions.

1. She called him because she needed help. _Did she call him because she needed help?_

2. The plane was late because of the weather. _____

3. They cried since it was a sad movie. _____

4. He has moved due to a rent increase. _____

5. We ate a lot because it was delicious. _____

9. Write a *Wh-* question with *Why* for each situation.

1. He likes fishing. _Why does he like fishing?_____

2. I feel tired. _____

3. She's going to the store. _____

4. They need a baby-sitter. _____

5. We were feeling sad. _____

6. He stayed home from work. _____

7. They've gone to New York. _____

8. I'm going to quit. _____

10. Write two questions for each situation. First write a *Wh-* question with *Why*. Then write a *Yes/No* question with an adverbial phrase or clause of reason. Make up your own reasons.

1. She laughed. _Why did she laugh?_____

   _Did she laugh because you told a joke?_____

2. He stayed home today. _____

   _____

3. He left his country. _____

   _____

4. They smiled. _____

   _____

5. They had a fight. _____

   _____

6. She cried. _____

   _____

Practice

11. Think about your family and friends. What strange, surprising, or puzzling things have they done? Write ten *Wh-* questions with *Why* about these things. Use your own paper.

Examples: Why does Irina paint her fingernails black?
Why has my girlfriend stopped writing to me?

SO/SUCH...THAT

SO . . . THAT				
	SO	ADJECTIVE/ADVERB	THAT	RESULT CLAUSE
He was	so	funny	that	he made everyone laugh.
I laughed		hard		I cried.

SUCH . . . THAT				
	SUCH	NOUN PHRASE	THAT	RESULT CLAUSE
It was	such	a good deal	that	I had to buy it.
They're		comfortable shoes		I wear them every day.

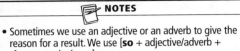

NOTES

• Sometimes we use an adjective or an adverb to give the reason for a result. We use [**so** + adjective/adverb + **that** + result clause].

• Sometimes we use a noun phrase to give the reason for a result. We use [**such** + noun phrase + **that** + result clause].

• EXCEPTION: We use **so** instead of **such** before noun phrases when the noun phrase contains the adjective **many**, **much**, **little**, or **few**: *He has so many papers that they cover his desk.*

• We often omit **that** after phrases with **so** or **such** in conversation and in informal writing: *I laughed so hard I cried.*

Rebecca and Sandy have been friends for
such a long time that they are like family.

Practice

12. Underline **so** + adjective/adverb + **that**. Circle **such** + noun phrase + **that**.

1. Sandy is so grateful that she almost starts to cry.

2. Sandy's problems with Jack were such an embarrassment that she kept them a secret.

3. The people at the shelter are so nice that Sandy feels comfortable with them.

4. The shelter is such a safe place that Sandy can relax there.

5. Rebecca and Kevin like Sandy so much that they want her to live in their apartment.

6. Rebecca is such a good friend that Sandy can tell her everything.

13. Write **so** or **such**.

1. It was <u>so</u> hot that we went swimming.

2. I was _____ tired that I didn't call you.

3. It was _____ a good movie that we want to see it again.

4. It was _____ crowded that we decided to leave.

5. He is _____ a fool that no one listens to him.

6. There were _____ many mosquitoes that we ran indoors.

14. Write statements with words and phrases from the boxes. Complete the statements with clauses of result.

He is They are	so	a good musician tall	that . . .
I cook It is	such	badly well	
They drive		kind people beautiful	

1. _He is so tall that most clothes don't fit him._____

2. _____

3. _____

4. _____

5. _____

6. _____

7. _____

8. _____

POWER Practice

15. Think about your friends. What are their good qualities? Write six sentences with **so...that** or **such...that**.

Examples: *My friend Jane is such a good listener that everyone wants to talk to her.*
My friend Steve is so handsome that women follow him on the street.

1. _____

2. _____

3. _____

4. _____

5. _____

6. _____

16. Think about your life. What things bother you? What things please you? Write six sentences with **so...that** or **such...that**. Use your own paper.

Examples: *My apartment is so messy that I have to do something about it.*
I have such nice neighbors that I really like my neighborhood.

DIRECT SPEECH

STATEMENTS	QUESTIONS
He said, **"It's time to study."** They said, **"The test was difficult."**	They asked, **"Is it time to leave?"** He asked, **"Where is Sally?"**

📝 **NOTES**

- Direct speech is a report of a person's exact words.
- We use quotation marks (**" "**) before and after the person's words. The final quotation marks come *after* the period or question mark.
- We use a comma before the first quotation mark: *He answered, "Yes, let's go."*
- We use a capital lettter for the first word in the quotation: *"Yes, let's go."*
- A sentence with direct speech has a verb like **say**, **ask**, or **answer**.

Anne asked, **"Would you like some ice cream?"**

Kevin answered, **"Yes, please."**

Practice

1. Check (✔) the sentences with direct speech. Underline the direct speech.

1. ✔ Rebecca asked, <u>"Who is it?"</u>

2. _____ Kevin answered her.

3. _____ Rebecca answered, "Come in."

4. _____ Rebecca said, "You and Uncle Brendan worked on the computer for hours last night."

5. _____ Kevin said, "It's amazing. He knows a lot about computers."

6. _____ Kevin told Rebecca about his idea.

2. Put the conversation in the correct order. Write the numbers on the lines.

a. _____ Anne said, "Two girls."

b. _____ Anne answered, "Kate's eight, and Erin's almost six."

c. _1_ Rebecca asked, "Is this your son, Michael?"

d. _____ Rebecca asked, "How old are they?"

e. _____ Anne answered, "Yes. He and his wife live in town."

f. _____ Rebecca asked, "Do they have any children?"

3. Put quotation marks (" ") around the direct speech. Put a comma before the first quotation mark.

1. Jane asked, **"**Where are you going?**"**

2. Tom said We need to buy milk at the store.

3. They asked When are we going to have the test?

4. The teacher answered The test will be tomorrow.

5. Yoko asked Are you going to the movies tonight?

6. Maria said I don't know.

4. Write questions or answers in direct speech. Use quotation marks (" ") and a comma before the first quotation mark.

1. David asked, **"**Are you going to go with us?**"**

Melanie answered, _"Yes, I am."_____

2. Pedro asked _____

Maria said, "No, I can't go. I have to study."

3. Reiko asked _____

Yoko answered, "To work."

4. Philip asked, "When are you going to leave?"

Michel said _____

5. The teacher asked _____

Susana answered, "I forgot it."

6. Gunther asked, "Will you marry me?"

Gretchen said _____

Practice

5. Write an interesting conversation between two members of your family. Write six sentences or more. Use direct speech. Use your own paper.

Examples: *My brother José said, "I am going to California."*
My sister Juanita asked, "What about your job?"

6. Ask a friend three questions. Write your questions and your friend's answers. Use your own paper.

Examples: *I asked, "Do you enjoy studying English?" Tranh said, "Yes, I do."*

PRESENT CONDITIONAL STATEMENTS

IF CLAUSE	RESULT CLAUSE
If you **speak** English every day,	your English **improves**.
If I **don't understand** the homework,	**then** I **call** a friend.

RESULT CLAUSE	IF CLAUSE
I **don't work** well	**if** I **don't eat** breakfast.
He **gets up** early	**if** he **doesn't go** to bed late.

> **NOTES**
> • A present conditional sentence tells the reason for a result. It has two clauses.
> • The **if** clause tells the reason. The result clause tells the result.
> • We use present tense verb forms in both the **if** clause and the result clause in a present conditional sentence.
> • The **if** clause can come before or after the result clause.
> • We use a comma after an **if** clause at the beginning of a sentence.
> • We sometimes use **then** at the beginning of a result clause when the result clause follows the **if** clause.

Brendan said, "**If** the demand for milk **goes** down, **then we're** in trouble."

7. Underline the reason and circle the result in each sentence.

1. If you live on a farm, you work hard every day.

2. If Brendan has time, he works on the computer.

3. Anne manages the farm if Brendan isn't there.

4. If seed prices go up, then farm profits go down.

5. Brendan lays off workers if the farm is in financial trouble.

6. If Rebecca thinks about her father, she feels sad.

8. Match the two parts of the sentences. Write the letters.

1. __e__ If it's a holiday,

2. _____ There is a danger of forest fires

3. _____ Water freezes

4. _____ If it's a hot day,

5. _____ If there is no rain,

a. if the temperature drops to 32°F.

b. then farmers are in trouble.

c. then we turn on the air conditioner.

d. if there is little rain.

✔**e.** then the stores are closed.

9. Complete the sentences with your own words. Use *result* clauses.

1. If the telephone rings, _I answer it._____

2. If my car doesn't start, _____

3. _____ if the weather is sunny.

4. If I hear loud music at night, _____

5. _____ if there's nothing in the refrigerator.

10. Complete the sentences with your own words. Use *if* clauses to tell the reasons.

1. I wear a heavy coat if _it's cold outside._____

2. If _____, they call the police.

3. She is happy if _____

4. If _____, it makes her mad.

5. He gets sick if _____

POWER Practice

11. What do you do in these situations? Answer the questions. Use present conditional sentences.

Example: *What do you do if you are sick? If I am sick, I call the doctor.*

1. What do you do if you are sick?

   _____

2. What do you do if you can't go to work or to class?

   _____

3. What do you do if your friend has a problem?

   _____

4. What do you do if you receive a gift?

   _____

12. Do you prefer living in the city or the country? Which one is better? Write six sentences with *if.* Use your own paper.

Examples: *If you live in the city, you are never bored. If you live in the country, life is too quiet.*

FUTURE CONDITIONAL STATEMENTS

IF CLAUSE	RESULT CLAUSE
If you **study** hard,	you **won't fail**.
If he **gets** a job next semester,	**then he'll take** night classes.

RESULT CLAUSE	IF CLAUSE
They'll call me	**if** they **need** help.
We **won't be** able to go	**if** the car **doesn't work**.

📝 NOTES

- A future conditional sentence tells the reason for a result in the future.
- We use present tense verb forms in the **if** clause.
- We use the future with **will** in the **result** clause.
- The **if** clause can come before or after the **result** clause.
- We use a comma after an **if** clause at the beginning of a sentence.
- We sometimes use **then** at the beginning of a result clause when the result clause follows the **if** clause.

Brendan said, "**If** you **stay** on the farm, **you'll be** a big help."

13. Underline the reason and circle the result in each sentence.

1. If the price of milk goes down, Brendan won't make much money.

2. If Brendan doesn't have enough money, then he won't fix the tractor.

3. Kevin will stay on the farm if it's OK with Brendan and Anne.

4. If Kevin stays on the farm, he'll work for Brendan.

5. Kevin said, "If I stay here, Rebecca will be able to return to school."

6. Rebecca won't return to school if she's worried about Kevin.

14. Match the two parts of the sentences. Write the letters.

1. __b__ If you eat junk food,

2. _____ If you exercise regularly,

3. _____ You won't be able to work well

4. _____ You'll have more energy

5. _____ If you eat a lot of candy,

a. you'll be stronger.

✔b. you'll gain weight.

c. if you eat good food.

d. you'll have problems with your teeth.

e. if you don't get enough sleep.

15. Complete the sentences with the correct form of the verb.

1. If he _fails_ (fail) this course, then he _won't graduate_ (not/graduate).

2. If Tom _____ (leave) now, I _____ (be) angry.

3. If it _____ (rain), we _____ (not/have) the picnic.

4. If the car _____ (cost) a lot of money, then I _____ (not/buy) it.

5. I _____ (give) them the message if I _____ (see) them.

6. He _____ (tell) us if he _____ (know) the answer.

16. Complete the following sentences. Add a reason or a result. Use your own words.

1. If she drives slowly, _she won't have an accident_ _____.

2. If he doesn't study, _____.

3. _____, then we'll get there on time.

4. We'll win the game _____.

5. If you need a ride to school, _____.

6. I won't go _____.

POWER Practice

17. What will happen if . . . ? Write five sentences. Make the result in one sentence become the reason in the next sentence.

Examples: *If I learn to speak English, I will get a good job. If I get a good job, I'll make a lot of money. If I make a lot of money, . . .*

1. _____
2. _____
3. _____
4. _____
5. _____

18. Give advice about how to learn English. Write six sentences with *if*. Use your own paper.

Examples: *If you learn three new words a day, your vocabulary will improve.*
If you speak English often, it will become easier.